Affiliate Marketing Mastery: The Ultimate Guide to Starting Your Online Business and Earning Passive Income

Unlock Profitable Affiliate Secrets, Boost Earnings with Expert Strategies, Top Niches, High-Performance Products, Innovative Tactics and Essential Tools for Success

Change Your Life Guru

Books by **Change Your Life Guru:**

Affiliate Marketing Mastery: *The Ultimate Guide to Starting Your Online Business and Earning Passive Income - Unlock Profitable Affiliate Secrets, Boost Earnings with Expert Strategies, Top Niches, High-Performance Products, Innovative Tactics and Essential Tools for Success*

Dropshipping Business Mastery: *The Ultimate Guide to Starting & Managing a Thriving Dropshipping Business - Skyrocket Your Income with Proven Strategies, Profitable Niches, and Unleash Powerful Marketing Tactics*

Etsy Store Mastery: *The Ultimate Guide to Building Your Own Etsy Empire - Learn Proven Strategies for Finding & Selling the Hottest Products, Building Your Brand, and Dominating Your Niche on Etsy*

Online Course Mastery: *The Ultimate Guide to Creating and Marketing Profitable Online Courses - Learn How to Find Your Niche, Create Engaging Content, and Succeed as an Online Course Creator*

Online Freelancing Mastery: *The Ultimate Guide to Making Money as an Online Freelancer - Unlock Proven Strategies to Monetize Your Skills and Talents, Market Yourself, and Go from Zero To Success*

Online Tutoring: *The Ultimate Guide to Creating a Profitable Online Tutoring Business – Become an Expert in Your Niche, Craft Engaging Sessions, Harness Powerful Marketing Strategies, and Profit from Your Expertise in the Digital Learning World*

Print on Demand Mastery: *The Ultimate Blueprint for Print on Demand Success - Unlock Actionable Tips & Strategies to Starting, Setting Up, and Marketing a Profitable Print on Demand Business*

Social Media Influencer: *The Ultimate Guide to Building a Profitable Social Media Influencer Career - Learn How to Build Your Brand, Create Viral Content, and Make Brands Beg to Pay for Your Lifestyle*

Subscription Business Model: *The Ultimate Guide to Building and Scaling A Predictable Recurring Income Business - Attract and Retain Loyal Subscribers, and Maximize Your Profitability with Proven Strategies and Best Practices*

YouTube Influencer: *The Ultimate Guide to YouTube Success, Content Creation, and Monetization Strategies - Build and Grow a Thriving YouTube Channel and Boost Engagement with Proven Techniques and Insider Secrets*

© Copyright 2023 - All rights reserved.

The content contained within this book may not be reproduced, duplicated or transmitted without direct written permission from the author or the publisher.

Under no circumstances will any blame or legal responsibility be held against the publisher, or author, for any damages, reparation, or monetary loss due to the information contained within this book, either directly or indirectly.

Legal Notice:

This book is copyright protected. It is only for personal use. You cannot amend, distribute, sell, use, quote or paraphrase any part, of the content within this book, without the consent of the author or publisher.

Disclaimer Notice:

Please note the information contained within this document is for educational and entertainment purposes only. All effort has been executed to present accurate, up to date, reliable, complete information. No warranties of any kind are declared or implied. Readers acknowledge that the author is not engaged in the rendering of legal, financial, medical or professional advice. The content within this book has been derived from various sources. Please consult a licensed professional before attempting any techniques outlined in this book.

By reading this document, the reader agrees that under no circumstances is the author responsible for any losses, direct or indirect, that are incurred as a result of the use of the information contained within this document, including, but not limited to, errors, omissions, or inaccuracies.

THANK YOU – A Gift For You!

THANK YOU for purchasing our book! *You could have chosen from dozens of other books on the same topic but you took a chance and chose this one.* As a token of our appreciation, we would like to offer you an exclusive **FREE GIFT BOX**. Your Gift Box contains powerful downloadable products, resources and tools that are the perfect companion to your newly-acquired book, and are designed to catapult you towards freedom and success.

To get instant access, just go to:
https://changeyourlife.guru/toolkit

Inside your Free Gift Box, you'll receive:

- **Goal Planners and Schedulers**: Map out manageable and actionable steps so you have clarity and are empowered with a clear roadmap to achieve every goal.

- **Expert Tips & Tricks:** Invaluable tips and strategies ready to apply to your life, or business, to accelerate your progress and reach your outcomes.

- **Exclusive Content:** Free bonus materials, resources, and tools to help you succeed.

- **New Freebies:** Enter your email address to download your free gift box and be updated when we add new Free Content, ensuring you always have the tools, information and strategies to sky-rocket your success!

Are you ready to supercharge your life? Download your gift box for FREE today! **[https://changeyourlife.guru/toolkit]**

Table of Contents

INTRODUCTION 1

CHAPTER 1: WHAT IS AFFILIATE MARKETING 3

   THE MAIN PLAYERS 3
      The Merchant 4
      The Affiliate Network 4
      The Affiliate Marketer 4
      Customer 5
   THE STAGES OF AFFILIATE MARKETING 5
   WHAT DO YOU NEED TO GET STARTED? 6
      Start Your Content Site 6
      Choose a Niche and Industry 6
      Research Products and Services 6
      Find Affiliate Programs 7
      Create Content 7
      Optimize Your Page and Track Ranks 7
   CHECKLIST 8

CHAPTER 2: THE DIFFERENT AFFILIATE MARKETING PROGRAMS ... 9

   WHAT EXACTLY ARE AFFILIATE PROGRAMS? 9
   HOW DO AFFILIATE PROGRAMS WORK? 9
   EXAMPLES OF AFFILIATE PROGRAMS 10
      ClickBank 10
      Commission Junction 10
      Amazon Associates 11
      GiddyUp 11
      Impact 11
      eBay Partner Network 12
      Awin 12
      Rakuten Affiliate 13
   CHOOSING THE RIGHT AFFILIATE PROGRAM 13
      How to Choose 13

CHOOSING THE BEST AFFILIATE PRODUCT	15
STARTING YOUR AFFILIATE MARKETER CAREER	17
Affiliate Marketing Platform	*18*
Choosing a Niche	*23*
TYPES OF AFFILIATE PROGRAMS	25
CREATING CONTENT	26
Tools to Improve Your Content	*29*
Tips on Creating Writing Content	*30*
Tips on Creating Video Content	*32*
GET CLICKS TO YOUR LINKS	37
CONVERTING CLICKS INTO SALES	38
CHECKLIST	41
CHAPTER 3: WHAT TYPE OF AFFILIATE MARKETER DO YOU WANT TO BE?	**43**
THE MAIN TYPES OF AFFILIATE MARKETING	43
Unattached Affiliate Marketing	*44*
Related Affiliate Marketing	*44*
Involved Affiliate Marketing	*44*
BEST MEDIUMS FOR AFFILIATE MARKETING	45
Influencer and Social Media Affiliate Marketing	*45*
Blogging and Affiliate Marketing	*46*
Mobile Affiliate Marketing	*47*
Coupon Affiliate Programs	*47*
Affiliate Email Marketing	*48*
Affiliate Marketing Incentive Programs (Loyalty Programs)	*49*
News Websites and Review Websites	*50*
WHAT TYPE OF AFFILIATE MARKETER DO YOU WANT TO BE?	50
Success Tips	*52*
CHECKLIST	54
CHAPTER 4: AFFILIATE MARKETERS AND TAXES	**55**
WHAT TAXES DO AFFILIATE MARKETERS PAY?	55
The Different Tax Forms	*56*
Tracing Your Taxable Income	*56*
Tax Deductions for Affiliate Marketers	*57*
TAX REGULATIONS OUTSIDE OF THE UNITED STATES	57

  Filing Taxes in the United Kingdom *57*
  Filing Taxes in Germany *58*
  Filing Taxes in Australia *58*
  Filing Taxes in Russia *59*
 CHECKLIST 59

CHAPTER 5: STRATEGIES TO KICKSTART YOUR AFFILIATE MARKETING 61

 BEGINNER STRATEGIES 62
  Shop Around for Best Commission Rates *62*
  Build Connections With Your Audience and Community *63*
  Find a Mentor *63*
  Diversify Your Affiliate Programs *63*
  Get Creative Promoting Products *63*
  Start Partnerships Directly With Brands *64*
  Add Affiliate Links Where Most Traffic Is Located *64*
  Customize Links for Different Countries *65*
  Marketing for Free *65*
  Share Content Everywhere *66*
  Become Data-Driven *66*
 ADVANCED AFFILIATE MARKETING STRATEGIES 66
  Owning All the Search Engine Results Page *66*
  Set Up Proper Affiliate Tracking *67*
  Get On-Page Optimization *68*
  Be More Efficient at Promoting Your Products and Services ... *69*
  Create an Affiliate Marketing Funnel *70*
  Building a More Efficient Email List *72*
  Choose Affiliate Programs With Recurring Commissions *72*
  Run Recurring Campaigns *73*
  Put More Effort on Items That Are Working Now *73*
 TIPS TO GET YOU STARTED 74
  Disclose Your Affiliate Links *74*
  Updating Your Content Regularly *75*
  Become an Influencer Marketer *75*
  Know Your Value *75*
 CHECKLIST 76

CHAPTER 6: TOOLS AND SOFTWARE FOR THE AFFILIATE MARKETER 78

FREE AFFILIATE TOOLS AND SOFTWARE 78
- Tools for Content Ideas 79
- Tools for Social Media and Email Marketing 80
- Tools for Link Tracking and Link Creation 80
- Tools for SEO 81
- Free Assets 83
- Free Tools for Ads and Optimization 83
- Free Tools for Content Editors 84

PAID AFFILIATE TOOLS AND SOFTWARE 84
- MobileMonkey 85
- Voluum 85
- AffJet 85
- AdPlexity 86
- Zeropark 86
- Flippa 87
- Unbounce 87
- Rebrandly 87
- ThirstyAffiliates 88
- Thrive Leads 88

AFFILIATE TOOLS FOR SPECIFIC PLATFORMS 88
- Tailwind 88
- Amazon Affiliate WordPress Plug-in 89
- MobileMonkey for SMS 89
- Pods by Quuu 89
- MeetEdgar 90
- Agorapulse 90
- Analisa.io 90
- PhantomBuster 90
- Brand24 91
- AddThis 91

CHECKLIST 92

CHAPTER 7: LAUNCHING YOUR CAMPAIGN 94

STEPS TO LAUNCH YOUR AFFILIATE MARKETING CAMPAIGN 94

    Pick a Traffic Source *94*
    Choose Offer Categories *95*
    Designing Landing Pages *96*
    Setting up Backend *96*
    Launching Your Campaign *97*
  OPTIMIZING YOUR AFFILIATE MARKETING CAMPAIGN 97
    Optimizing for Quality of Traffic *97*
    Optimizing for Conversions *100*
  OTHER TIPS TO OPTIMIZE YOUR CAMPAIGN 101
  CHECKLIST 103

CHAPTER 8: ADVERTISING YOUR CAMPAIGN 104

  HOW TO CREATE AN AD? 104
    Choose Your Target Audience *104*
    Choosing the Platform for Your Ads *105*
    Decide on Your Budget *105*
    Create Your Message *106*
    Get People Talking *107*
    Decide What You Are Doing First *108*
    Create Test Ads *108*
    Creating Assets *109*
    Determine How to Measure Your Progress *109*
    Launching Your Ad *110*
  CHECKLIST 135

CONCLUSION 137

Introduction

Have you ever read a blog that mentions an *affiliate link*? And as you scroll through the article, you're linked to a product or service? That is the most basic form of affiliate marketing that most people will come across. At its core, affiliate marketing is when someone gets a commission for advertising a service or product on behalf of another business, most commonly through an affiliate link (hyperlink). Every time that link is clicked on, or the customer purchases the product or service from there, the marketer gets a commission.

Although we used a blog article as an example, affiliate marketing can be found in almost every online medium, including websites, podcasts, social media content, and so on. Assume you operate a fashion blog and are examining a pair of shoes to better understand how an affiliate program works. You've joined an affiliate program (or a business approaches you to advertise their products), and you've obtained an affiliate link that you post to your blog. When your readers click on it, it takes them to the merchant's website where the shoes can be purchased. These links contain a tracking code, which allows the affiliate network or program to know where the click came from. The reader purchases the shoes, and the company records that the customer came from your blog and affiliate link; once the transaction is credited, you get paid your commission.

We will look at different types of affiliate marketing throughout this book. There is:

- connected affiliate marketing
- unattached affiliate marketing
- engaged affiliate marketing

However, as you shall discover, affiliate marketing is much more than that. Don't worry if none of this makes sense yet. This book will teach you everything you need to get started!

Affiliate marketing is an excellent method to generate revenue from your website, blog, or social media posts. You are not simply writing about or advertising a product or service; you may earn money from it. This changed not just the way numerous written mediums, such as blogs and social media postings, but also how advertising operated.

Affiliate marketing has numerous advantages and brings many rewards, not only as an additional source of income. For instance, it gives you access to a very large market, and while you can earn, you can also advertise at a low cost, partner up with great brands, grow your social media following, and it has a very low risk and a low entry barrier too!

Chapter 1:

What Is Affiliate Marketing

So now that you have an idea of what affiliate marketing is, let's take a closer look at it, and what it means to be an affiliate marketer.

Whatever content medium you use, whether it is a blog, email, social media posts, or anything in between, every time you promote a company's service or product and it leads to a sale, you gain a commission. So, what you're essentially doing is promoting somebody else's products or services, and you get a commission if a customer purchases that product or service through your reference.

The best way to join an affiliate program is to sign up for it. There are many types of programs, with the main distinctions being the various services and products they use, the amount of commissions they pay, and how they pay it. If you prefer, you can also work with single companies that you handpick.

As an affiliate marketer, you will create content (whatever content you prefer), join an affiliate program, or contact companies that you'd like to work for and include their products or services in your content so potential customers can become aware of them or click on the links and potentially drive sales of that product or service. Now, there are several components within the cycle of affiliate marketing.

The Main Players

If you're just starting out, it's reasonable that some of the terms that you see thrown around when researching affiliate marketing might get you a little confused, plus many of those terms can actually be interchangeable. But there are four main players in the affiliate marketing business that form the basis of everything. These are the merchant, the affiliate network, the affiliate, and the customer.

The Merchant

The merchant, sometimes known as the seller, the advertiser, the marketer, or the brand, is the owner of the service or product that you will be advertising and that pays you a commission. You will have to drive traffic to their website in order for them to increase their sales and for you to get a commission. These could be a store, a retailer of pretty much anything, or a company selling a service, such as a subscription, software, etc.

The Affiliate Network

This is the company that acts as the middleman between you and the merchant. The merchant reaches out to the affiliate network to promote some of their products or services. This way, they can simply focus on what they are creating, and you can simply focus on how to promote the merchant's products or services.

The affiliate network also has affiliate tracking software that allows the merchant to measure their promotional partnerships with you. So, essentially, it tracks down how many customers used the links in all of the merchants' partnerships.

There are two main types of affiliate networks: direct and advertising. In direct affiliate marketing, the affiliate marketer directly posts a link for the merchant's product or service, while in an advertising affiliate marketing situation, there's an advertisement of the product or service that directs the consumer to it.

The Affiliate Marketer

The affiliate marketer, also known as a partner or publisher, is you. The job of an affiliate marketer is to promote the products or the services through whatever medium of work they do and drive sales towards the websites of the products and services. Every time there's a sale that comes from the affiliate marketer's link to the merchant's website and a sale happens, the marketer gets a commission.

As we've already mentioned, there are quite a few ways to promote these services and products, such as through blog posts, social media posts, email, etc. Along these lines, there's something called "traffic sources." This essentially refers to the source of the traffic to the advertiser's website. Now, there are several types of traffic sources in affiliate marketing, such as mobile traffic, social traffic, or search traffic. These are quite easy to understand; for instance, mobile traffic is all the traffic that came from mobile devices, while social traffic is all the traffic that came from social media pages. But perhaps more important than that is the quality of the traffic sources, which we will talk about later in the book.

Customer

A customer, or consumer, is the person who purchases the products and services. In this particular case with affiliate marketing, they would click on one of the affiliate links that would direct them to the page of the product or service of the merchant, and they would purchase it there.

The Stages of Affiliate Marketing

We've already seen how affiliate programs work, but let's review it so we can tie it up with the next section to make a little more sense. Through your content, you show an advertisement from a merchant about a certain product or service; once the customer clicks on it (through a tracking link), they will be led to the merchant's product or service page. When the customer purchases what you are advertising, the affiliate network saves the purchase and where the customer came from. Once the transaction is done, you will get a commission.

So, how do you get started? It's simpler than you might think. The first thing you need to do is create your content. So, if you're a blogger, you will have to create a blog. If you're an influencer, you have to create a social media page, and so on. You will have to choose a niche or industry to operate in since your content has to be somehow related to this industry or niche.

Here, you will have to do your due diligence on the products and niches that you want to promote, but we will talk about this later on. You will then have to sign up for an affiliate program or contact companies if you want to work only with single companies. Then, all you have to do is create content in any form you'd like. Obviously, there's a little more work than this, but these are the various steps you will have to take.

What Do You Need to Get Started?

While starting in affiliate marketing is not a complicated thing, it does require some patience and hard work.

Start Your Content Site

Whether it's a website, blog, social media page, or anything else, the very first thing you need to do is create a place where you can post content for people to see. This is the only way possible for you to get into affiliate marketing because that's how you link to pages of products and services from the merchant.

Choose a Niche and Industry

Then, you will have to narrow down the potential customers you want to bring to your content site. This is important so you can cater to a target audience and create your content around that. This way, it becomes a lot easier to find products and services to promote.

This will also help you grow your own audience and get more commissions from promoting products and services.

Research Products and Services

Once you've chosen an industry and niche, you need to conduct your due diligence and find products or services that you can promote. This is the time to create a spreadsheet and evaluate your options. We will go into more detail about this later in the book.

Find Affiliate Programs

Here you are also required to perform research on affiliate programs that you can join. There are many that you can choose from, and we will also dedicate a chapter to them. However, the most important thing is to research. Look at the companies they work with and the commission they pay.

Some of the most popular affiliate marketing websites include ClickBank, CJ Affiliate, and GiddyUp, but there are many more with more specific niches that might work better with what you want to do.

Create Content

This part is crucial if you want to grow your audience, which is also vital if you want to earn more through affiliate marketing. Content is the core of what you want to do; without good content, you won't have a business at all. There are many types of content, but only some will be relevant for the niche and products that you are creating content around.

If you don't have particularly good writing skills, hiring a freelance writer can be of great help. Alternatively, you can research the different methods out there for writing compelling texts.

Optimize Your Page and Track Ranks

Optimizing your page or pages for SEO will make them more visible for people, which will generate traffic and eventually more commission. Here, you can develop some strategies that will increase this, such as an email marketing strategy. It's also important that you check your ranking on Google to see how you're doing.

In the following chapter, we will go in-depth regarding the different affiliate programs there are, what products and niches they cater to, and how you can pick the best products or services on the market to help you grow your audience.

Checklist

	Start your content site
	Choose your industry and niche
	Research products and services
	Find affiliate programs
	Create content
	Optimize your page and track your rank

Chapter 2:

The Different Affiliate Marketing Programs

Affiliate marketing programs come in many different shapes and forms, and that's exactly what we will talk about in this chapter. You shouldn't simply pick a program that has a product that you like, or you shouldn't choose another just because they say they cater to your niche. While that is a good starting point for your research, there is a lot more to it before you can choose it. In fact, you don't have to pick just one. However, let's start from the beginning.

What Exactly Are Affiliate Programs?

Affiliate programs, also known as "associate programs," are a platform (third party) that assists affiliate marketers in locating products and services with which they can collaborate. Simply put, once the marketer signs up for the platform, they arrange a partnership and start to promote the services or products of the merchant.

How Do Affiliate Programs Work?

After the partnership is created and the marketer has chosen what brand, products, or services to promote, the affiliate program creates a link that the marketers can use and share on their content for the customers to click on, which leads them to the merchant's web page for the product or service. Once a sale is made through this link, the marketer receives a commission.

Examples of Affiliate Programs

While there are many different affiliate programs out there and the best depends on the products or services that you choose to advertise, we will give you some examples of the most popular affiliate programs at the time of writing. In the next section, we will then give you some tips on how you can pick the best program for your needs.

ClickBank

This is an affiliate program that has been around for quite some time, and it's one of the most popular choices within the affiliate marketing industry. This is because they have a wide array of companies working with them, so it caters to many different types of affiliate marketers.

Some of their most popular categories, for example, are sports, travel, home improvements, entertainment, gardening, investing, or business. So, as you can see, there's a lot to choose from. Like most affiliate programs, to use ClickBank, you need to sign up and create an account. Their commission varies, but it's usually between 50% and 70%. They pay every week or every two weeks, and you can get paid through direct deposit, wire transfer, check, or Payoneer.

Commission Junction

Commission Junction, or simply CJ, is also another company that has been in the industry for more than 20 years. They claim to have more than 500 companies that they work with, making them one of the first choices of many merchants and marketers. They are also a "generalist" when it comes to the different companies that they work with, so they have a wide selection of industries.

It's definitely a place that you want to look at when researching your affiliate programs. They usually offer between 5% and 10% commission, but it all depends on the advertiser, and they pay you within 2 weeks to 20 days of the end of the month. They also pay you through Payoneer, checks, or direct deposits.

Amazon Associates

This might surprise you, but Amazon Affiliates—from the giant tech company Amazon—wasn't created after all the success the company had. Their affiliate program started back in 1996, and it was one of their first business models and one of the first affiliate programs in the industry.

Obviously, they cater to Amazon customers now, but because of their success both in selling and in getting people to sell on the platform, this can be a great opportunity for you. It goes without saying that they also have a wide list of niches and products under their belt. Their commission is between 1% and 20%, and the payout methods they use are direct deposit, check, or Amazon Gift Card, so it's a little more limited in this area when compared to other affiliate programs. Another disadvantage of Amazon Associates is that they usually only pay after two months.

GiddyUp

GiddyUp is an excellent choice for those who are just getting started because it provides excellent tools and an easy-to-use interface that can assist you with the fundamentals. They have around 150 brands they work with, so it's a little more limited than some of the other affiliate programs on this list, but they also have a more curated industry list, spanning from health to electronics to traveling. They also have great guides that can help you with your marketing campaigns and great data reports. This way, you can simply monitor your performance and understand the things that you need to improve.

They pay on the 1st and 15th of every month, and besides checks and ACH, they also offer foreign bank transfers. Their commission, however, varies widely depending on your type of referral.

Impact

Impact is very selective with the brands that they work with, and it's perhaps the only place where you can find brands such as Adidas or Uber. Their biggest advantage is their use of automation tools that can make your life a lot easier, help you make more sales, and run a smooth marketing campaign. This affiliate program is free to join, and all you have to do is sign up and create an account.

Because the brands they work with come from a variety of industries, their commission rates vary greatly. However, unlike other affiliate programs, you can choose when to get paid. Another advantage is the payout method that allows you to use PayPal as well as direct transfer, or BACS.

If you want easy access to your money and a diversified payment method, Impact is a great affiliate program to go for.

eBay Partner Network

The eBay Partner Network, much like Amazon Associates, is a place where you can sign up and become an affiliate for eBay. Furthermore, the eBay Partner Network pays one of the highest commission rates in the affiliate industry, ranging from 50% to 70%.

They also provide you with many different tools to market products on eBay in a simple manner. Another difference in the eBay Partner Network is that you would be working directly with eBay and the products they sell. Like Amazon Associates, there are many sellers who can help you increase your sales, but they are all focused on products. They pay on the 10th of each month, as long as you have at least $10. These sellers pay through direct deposit and PayPal.

Awin

Awin is another great affiliate program that beginners like to use because it allows you to connect with the platform, not only with your website but also with almost all social media pages that you might have. There's a $5 deposit if you want to join the program, but you can get that back once you get your first payment. They work with more than 20,000 companies and brands, and you can check out all of them through their website. The commission varies depending on the seller, and they can pay through BACS, ACH, or international wire transfer on the 1st or 5th of each month, but you need to have at least $20.

Rakuten Affiliate

Rakuten Affiliate is one of the top three affiliate programs in the world, so it's definitely worth having a look at. They work with over 2,500 brands in the most diverse industries. They also have a really simple application process once you find the products you want to promote.

One of the different aspects of Rakuten Affiliates is that the brands themselves are quite involved in the screening of the promoters, so they can also decide if you are a good fit for their brand or not.

Commission rates vary widely depending on the brand and product you are promoting; they pay every 90 days and you have to have a minimum of $50. They also accept direct deposit or check as a payout method.

Choosing the Right Affiliate Program

The first thing that you should do is simply do a search (through Google) and try to combine the terms "affiliate marketing" with the niche or products you are looking for. Anything that comes up in the search might be a good starting point. After you've got your list, continue by checking their website. This is also where you can become an affiliate marketer with the company, but before that, you should have a look at the features they offer as well as their brand partners.

Alternatively, you can also check affiliate programs' directories. They have huge databases that you can explore and find what you need. Affiliate Seeking is an example of such a directory.

How to Choose

By visiting the affiliate program's website, you can get an idea of how reputable the company is. However, you need to dig a little deeper to fully understand their reputation and if there are common issues reported by other users. Obviously, if you partner with brands that offer great services and products, your customers will certainly be happy, as will your audience. This makes your audience and your business grow. This and a great affiliate strategy can increase your reputation and help you get higher and higher commissions.

There are many ways to check an affiliate program's reputation. You can do it through Google Reviews, TrustPilot, or any other review website. Social media is another great place to check. There, you can look for reviews, their activity, or active users to get a better idea of how the customers perceive the company.

When choosing a service or a product, it's best to pick one that you've used before. Since you're promoting it, having used it will give you a much better insight into what you are going to say and make it far more engaging than just writing or talking about something that you've heard other people talking or writing about. Even if you haven't tried the service or product but you really want to promote it, you can still do it if you really learn about it. Alternatively, you can actually buy it and test it yourself. Essentially, the more you know about a product or service, the better you are at promoting it.

Obviously, you will want to promote something that is related to your niche. So, if you have a blog related to sportswear, you will want to sell products or services related to that. If you market yourself and your page or blog as having a certain niche and then sell products or services that are unrelated to it, it will make your audience drop your content. However, you can always get creative if you really want to promote something that doesn't fit your niche, but don't do it at all times.

You will also want to look for affiliate programs that can get you competitive commission rates. There are a few different types of commissions, such as pay-per-action or pay-per-sale. You may receive a commission if the customer performs certain actions under the "pay-per-action" payout model. This could be as simple as visiting a website, purchasing something, filling out a form or poll, and so on. With pay-per-sale, as the name suggests, you get a commission every time a customer purchases something from the merchant's website through your link. These commissions tend to be a little higher than the pay-per-action ones, but also a little harder to achieve. You need to research the percentage of commissions and find out what works best for you. Offering a custom link option is also a great feature most affiliate programs have nowadays, but you want to make sure they support that feature. Essentially, instead of a long, unreadable URL link, you can customize it to a shorter one or even incorporate it into your content.

There's a very important factor to consider when choosing an affiliate program, and that is cookie duration. This refers to how long your affiliate link is valid. Usually, the duration of cookies varies between 10 and 30 days, but you need to know for sure since any purchase made through the link after the cookie expires will not give you any commission. Essentially, you want long-term expiration for cookies, but the affiliate program website should have all the information you need.

The more efficient an affiliate program is, the better for you. And one that uses tracking sales technology is exactly what you should be looking for. This not only makes it easier for the affiliate program to manage their business, but it also makes the marketer's life seamless when it comes to understanding their performance and things that they should improve. You can also use such a tracking system to see how many times your audience clicked on the links on your page or how many paying customers came from your website.

Choosing the Best Affiliate Product

Before you choose a product, you first need to look at the market niche. Make a list of all the products or services that you might be interested in promoting, then take an overall look to find out what type of niche most interests you.

You might also have to cut some off the list based on other parameters, such as the ones that earn you less commission. A simple Google search will give you an estimate of the average commission per niche. You also need to do this for products.

Once you've got a few market niches down, it's time to go a little more in depth. How do you feel about promoting that particular niche? Do you think your skills and interests will allow you to do that on a regular basis? The more you know about it and are interested in it, the easier it gets for you.

Then, you will have to analyze market demand. Essentially, this is the demand for a certain product, service, or niche. To summarize, the higher the demand for something, the more money you can potentially make. Here, you should aim for a service or product that helps solve an issue or is currently trending (although this might not last for a long time). However, ideally, you should look for services and products that solve a problem and are so-called "evergreen." This means that they are not a passing fad, but because this might be hard to achieve at the beginning, starting out with trendy products just to build your audience is a good strategy. Evergreen means they will sell well all year and for many years to come.

Let's now go through the different parameters that you need to consider to choose the best product or service to promote. At this point, you've already scouted the different affiliate marketplaces and chosen the ones to go with. This will make it easier for you to choose what you want to promote. Ideally, you would individually sign up for all the affiliate programs that interest you so that you have a larger range of products or services that you can promote. Affilitizer is a Chrome add-on that can help you look for marketplaces and direct you to their websites.

Now that you have a few products or services in your preferred niche, you can use Google again to find out who their competitors are. It is critical that you understand what other products or services may compete with yours in order to be better prepared. You can simply go to Google and use the "vs." auto-suggest feature to find this. All you have to do is type in the search bar "your product or service vs.," and Google will suggest to you, in this case, a competitive product or service.

Once you've chosen a couple of good products or services within your niche, you can expand your search by using alternative keywords. All you have to type in on Google is "product or service + alternative." This way, you can find out about similar products and even add them to your list.

In order to increase your conversion rate, promoting the best-selling products or services in your niche might be a great start since this is what defines a successful affiliate campaign from one that doesn't. Once again, having used the product or service can really make a difference in how you promote it, so make sure when it comes to products, you've tested them and used the services, even if it was just a trial. The criteria to choose a product or service should be in line with the niche and the way you conduct your affiliate strategy. Make sure whatever you choose to promote fits your style of promotion, whether this is through a blog, a social media page, a video, etc.

Because the ability to track your affiliate referrals is critical for profit, you must always ensure that these work. It might not be integral for you to choose the product, but it's always good to remember to check that everything is in order. Check the links in your content to make sure they lead you to the right page and to see if the merchant recognizes your affiliate link.

Lastly, while picking some products or services that are trending might be a good beginner's strategy, always following the crowd is not something that you want to always do, especially when you've acquired enough experience and built a solid audience. You will eventually have to find your own hidden gems within your niche, although the ability to do that will come with experience.

Starting Your Affiliate Marketer Career

Now that you know the basics of affiliate marketing, how do you start your career? While we will present the way you can kick-start your career in a few simple steps, this requires some work on your behalf. Starting your affiliate marketing career, much like any other process, such as a business, requires some planning. However, you don't have to spend as much money upfront to actually start earning with affiliate marketing, and you definitely won't need employees, either. Nonetheless, having a plan will make your life a lot easier and increase your chances of success in the industry.

Assuming you've already chosen a niche and a few products that you would like to promote, we can skip ahead and go straight to which platform you want to use and how to optimize your content for search engines.

Affiliate Marketing Platform

There are many different ways you can create content, but not all are suitable to your marketing style, the products or services that you want to promote, or even your own skill sets. Here, we will give you a few ideas that you can explore.

Blogs

Blogs are perhaps the most popular platforms when it comes to affiliate marketing because they offer you diversity in the type of content that you want to promote. Because blogs are a writing medium, they can be used for anything that falls under the category of writing, such as product and service reviews, product and service roundups, or product and service comparisons, to name a few.

Product and service reviews are one of the most popular ways to use blogs to promote since online reviews help most people choose their products and services. According to a recent study, around 97% of consumers use online reviews to help them accurately choose what to purchase. One thing to keep in mind when doing these is to keep it accurate and honest. Don't be biased, thinking that you will get more commissions; otherwise, your audience won't have trust in your reviews.

Product and service comparisons are another great way to create content that people are interested in. Essentially, you'd be comparing similar products or services so that readers could easily identify the advantages and disadvantages of specific products and services if they were to purchase them. While it is not as detailed as a product or service review, you must still highlight and compare the key points of each. When it comes to comparisons, you want to make it as easy as possible for the reader to observe the advantages and disadvantages of the product or service you are comparing. Depending on the product or service, there are many factors that you can compare, but things such as price or manufacturer should always be included.

Product roundups work better with products, and essentially, you're gathering certain items that can combine with one another. This way, you can lead your audience to more than one product. However, if you just have one link, make sure you make that product your main one to drive more sales. Usually, clothing and accessory brands come up with roundups to make it easier to sell certain products, and if this is the type of product you're into, then creating this type of content can really be beneficial to growing your audience. However, roundups are not only a unique clothing brand thing; if you're creative enough, you can roundup pretty much anything, even services such as Minecraft hosting servers, for instance. You want to find the theme that connects with your readers and build your roundup from there.

Email Marketing

While email marketing takes time to build, it's definitely one of the most effective methods to increase your repeat sales. What you want to do with email marketing is drive traffic to the merchant's website or link it to your content. However, different affiliate networks have different rules regarding email marketing, so it's best for you to have a look at them first. For instance, Amazon doesn't allow you to attach affiliate links to email marketing, so this is not a good method if you're using such an affiliate program. You can get creative and send newsletters instead, where you can post links to the merchant's website or your own content website, for instance. Either way, the most important thing when it comes to email marketing is continuous, high-quality content and not simply advertising for the sake of advertising.

Tutorials

Tutorials are most often video-based type of content that show how a product or service is used. This helps your audience make a decision since they are more connected to the product or service and know exactly how to use it. You will have to place your video in context and create a narrative, such as how to use a certain function of a service or how to use the product for a certain thing. Either way, what you want to achieve is being able to recommend the product and how well it works.

Resource Pages

Resource pages are exactly what their name suggests: A place where your audience can find everything they need in a single place. Like a roundup page, a resource page should have an underlying theme and help the reader get to their goal, whatever that is.

This could be anything within your niche, such as gardening, baking, or home improvements, for example. It's very important that you understand what you're talking about when you create a resources page since, apart from certain necessary tools, there's not really a "buying intent" behind a resources page. In this case, high-quality content is your best shot at increasing conversion rates.

Ebooks

When the content of what you want to talk about is far too big, your best options are a series of articles or an ebook. Many prefer ebooks because they gather all the information in one place, making it easier to navigate. Ebooks work extremely well with email marketing lists because you can simply send them to your audience. While you can earn money from an ebook, you can also promote more than one product or service, so you have more than one revenue stream working on your behalf.

The only disadvantage is that ebooks take some time to write (or money if you want to pay a writer to do it), but they are certainly a great way to promote products or services in great detail.

Videos

Videos are another great medium for creating content. They are much more persuasive when it comes to getting people to follow a link because it's like you're speaking to them face-to-face instead of writing words on a page. If you're a good speaker, then videos might be the best option for you. You have plenty of different types of content that you can use with videos, from reviews to vlogs or even how-to videos. Your personality and the type of products or services you're promoting will dictate what type of videos you make.

Obviously, YouTube is the largest online platform when it comes to video content, and its affiliate marketing section makes it a gold mine if you're successful in bringing people to follow your page. But, of course, with extremely successful platforms, the competition increases too. Although there are other platforms that you should consider, such as Instagram Reels or TikTok, since they are growing in popularity.

If you need to engage people, videos are perhaps the best possible options out there, but your content has to be short and to the point, or you might lose your audience.

Gift Guides

Gift guides are an excellent choice as long as there's a celebration. Essentially, gift guides are a selection of recommendations for gifts that have a common goal; this could be a theme, the occasion, the budget, etc.

For example, "10 gift ideas under $30 for her on Valentine's." This is quite a popular request once Valentine's Day comes around and usually brings a higher conversion rate than other mediums.

Now, we can separate gift guides into two categories: guidance and convenience. Gift guides that fall into the "guidance" section have more to do with review and recommendation, which many of your readers seek. These have a high rate of conversion because your audience believes you've already done the work they should have done in selecting good gifts. When it comes to convenience, they also make it a lot easier for the audience to choose, which makes their selection process a lot smoother. Here, you will have to write important information such as size (if it's a product), price, or ratings.

Affiliate Landing Pages

Landing pages, as you might be aware, have a single purpose: to contain a call to action (CTA) and to convert readers and your audience into paying customers. That's their whole purpose, and they are designed in that way. Traffic to these landing pages usually comes from social media pages, email directories, or organic searches. Affiliate landing pages are, most of the time, the last step in a broader marketing campaign that prepares the audience for conversion, and because of that, the landing page should never aim to be the very first page the audience has contact with but the last push to get them to purchase the product or service.

Buyer's Guides

Some readers are looking for a buyer's guide, or "ultimate guide," as many are called, about a product or service. These are extremely comprehensive guides that allow your audience to understand everything they should know before making their purchase. While these guides can focus on the product or service, they are more often written to focus on a certain activity, such as "how to grow perfect grass in your garden," and from there, you will not only have to explain the whole process to your audience, but you also need to help them choose the best tools and tell them everything they need in terms of materials, etc.

After reading a buyer's guide, your audience should know everything they need to perform that activity.

Case Studies

To use case studies as a medium to promote products or services, you need to be able to convey a story, since these are based on real-life examples that might impact your audience and convert them into buyers. The stories you tell must include the product or service you're promoting as the main reference, and they have to solve a real-life problem.

This makes it a lot more relatable to your readers because they can then associate a problem with the solution that you're presenting. Even if that particular problem is not something that bothers them much, they have a solution right in front of them for when it does come around.

Social Media Posts

Nowadays, social media is where everyone is, so it's only normal that most of the promoting and marketing happen on those platforms. Any social media post promoting something is a piece of content, whether it is a picture, a video, or text, and you can really get creative with those. Now, the content is different for every platform because of the way these are built and the audience they cater to, so depending on the service or product you're promoting, the social media platform has to be chosen carefully.

Social media posts are a great way to get people engaged with the product or service, although you have to be on social media a lot more consistently. This means that you have to constantly create content in order to expand your audience and build trust.

Curations

Curations, like gift guides, are a selection of products, although they may be specific and not themed for a special occasion. Although curations might be similar to roundups, they try to give a much more personal feel to the potential customer. They are usually much more in-depth than roundups, too, and they often include the performance of the product compared to that of other similar products.

So, when creating a product curation, consider how you can make your content more personalized to increase conversion.

Choosing a Niche

While you might want to try and convert as many people as you can, going for several niches is never a great idea because it's quite hard to create content that caters to several types of people, or niches. That is why most affiliate marketers concentrate their efforts on one or two niches (usually related to one another).

Choosing the right niche is not an easy thing to do, but it's an essential step that you need to take to start building an audience. The question to ask yourself is: "how do I choose a great niche that will make my products or services sell?"

As we've previously mentioned, you should be interested in the niche, or you won't be happy doing it in the long run; the niche should also have consent from people, evaluate the competition, and look for affiliate networks that cater to that niche.

Once you've gone through these steps, you will be closer to finding your niche and your product or service. But let's go through the main steps to finding your niche. The first thing you need to do is research and brainstorm.

Websites such as Quantcast allow you to see the ranking of different websites on the internet, such as the "top 100" or "top 200" most visited. These websites' niches are clearly visible here. This could be travel, healthcare, clothing, etc. Whatever it is, you can get a much better idea of what most people are interested in on the internet, which will help you narrow down some niches. Quora is an excellent website to use to understand what questions people have and what they look for. For instance, if you type in Quora niches such as travel or healthcare, you will be presented with the main questions about those niches. Here, you should thrive on grabbing those questions or problems people have, creating content, and promoting services or products that help solve them. The more you scroll down through Quora, the more repeated questions you will see, and from there, you will understand what the people's main doubts are regarding that niche. If nothing relevant comes up when you search on Quora, you can go back to the audience-insight website and look for another category.

Then, you have to make sure the niche you've found is worthy. To do this, you have to use an affiliate program, such as ClickBank, to test it. You need to know if you are able to monetize the niche before you start putting effort into building an audience. ClickBank is just an example; there are many other affiliate networks that you can use. However, we will give you an example using ClickBank, but the process with any other affiliate network should be similar. To start testing the niche, go to "affiliate marketplace" on the platform. Then, you have two options: to simply type on the search bar to find products or to click on the drop-down menu and browse the categories. After you've selected the niche or category, you will have the results in front of you. On the left side of the screen, you will have filters to refine your searches a little better. If you sort the results by "gravity," you will get the sales per niche of every product on the page. Now, all you have to do is find a product that sells well for an average price, which will appear on the right side of each product.

To make sure your niches are good and you can start investing in them, you should check them with Adwords to understand what the usual cost-per-click on keywords is for that specific niche. When finding out the cost-per-click, you are trying to understand your competition, how much they bid, and who they are. You can do all of that with a tool that we've already mentioned previously: Google Adwords' Keyword Planner. Simply search for a new keyword and type in the niche you want to find out about. You can type in different variations of the niche you want to research at the same time. From here, you can click on "get ideas." The results will give you the average number of monthly searches and indicate the type of competition you'd be facing if you were to choose that niche or its variations. They also recommend the amount of the bid you should pay to give you an idea.

After you've found the perfect niche for you, you will be able to start selling. Now, of course, you need to know how to sell and promote the products, but that all depends on your ability to make people purchase products or services.

Types of Affiliate Programs

We've already talked about the steps you need to follow to choose the right affiliate program. But, we still need to talk about the different types of affiliate programs there are, and this might help you categorize the differences and help you pick the right one.

We can divide the types of affiliate programs into three different categories: high-paying/low-volume, low-paying/high-volume, and high-paying/high-volume. Each has different advantages and disadvantages depending on the products or services you choose to promote.

Let's start with high-paying/low-volume programs. These types of programs can get you really high commissions, but there are not that many buyers. If you are already established in the niche, this might be a great option, but if you're still building your audience, then it might be hard for you to make sales. These programs are also very selective and niched, so your products or services have to be quite specific.

The low-paying/high-volume type of programs are, as you might have already guessed, low-paying commissions, but there is a lot of demand for that product or service. But it also means that you need to sell quite a bit in order to make a significant profit.

Lastly, high-paying and high-volume programs are those that have quite popular services or products and also a lot of demand. But of course, these types of programs are quite hard to come by, but if you do your research properly, you might be able to find such a gold mine.

Creating Content

Content is the most important thing when it comes to affiliate marketing, and for that, the very first thing you should be doing is defining and planning your content marketing goals. This should be done even before you decide what you're going to create.

In this case, your main goal for creating content should be getting higher volumes of traffic through your website or social media pages, expanding your audience, and ultimately achieving higher conversions to make sales. Understanding exactly what your goals are is very important when it comes to planning and, later on, creating your content. Because the first goal is to steer more traffic your way, you want your content to get mentioned in larger places such as other bigger publications, larger social media pages, etc. While this might take some time, if you constantly create good content and promote it, it will eventually appear in major publications and increase the traffic on your website.

However, for that to happen, you need to perform your research and completely understand who your audience is. Now that you've found out your goal, you need to understand who is going to read, listen to, or watch your content. You need to research the demographics of the audience you want to persuade. You will have to look at the quality and traits of your potential audience, and you can achieve that through creating a buyer's persona, or in this case, an audience persona. This will help you realize who your audience is and aid you in creating content that is more engaging for that type of audience.

A buyer's persona is a fictional representation of your ideal audience, and the goal here is for you to get inspiration when creating your content to be able to relate to them. You want to give them traits, describe what they do on a daily basis, their education, what they do to pass the time, etc. Other important factors to consider are the platforms they use to search for products or services. This could be Google, Reddit, Quora, etc. How long do they spend on social media? Or what social media do they use?

You should be able to answer all of those questions to fully understand who your audience is and what they want in terms of content. If you're right, you will be able to bring more traffic to your website or social media page and convert some of those visitors into paying customers.

As we've previously discussed, there are many ways to create content. But one of the most popular ones is through a blog. We will write down a few ways that you can make your writing better to create content, but the first thing you should be doing is updating your current content if you have already published it.

Almost all content can be made great with a few changes, and it can save you a lot of time. Have another look at your content goal and try to tweak your current content to be in alignment with your current goals. Focus on three important things to accomplish this regardless of your goals: evergreen, engagement, and events. Evergreen content means that you should write about something that will still be relevant in years to come. Engagement means keeping your audience interested in what you're writing and also creating content around important events such as industry events, for example.

Writing about personal experience is something you should do when creating any type of content. This is exactly what we mean when we say to get your hands on the product or service you want to promote and use it. Talking about something that you have no experience with is a little more complicated. Ideally, you would be testing this product or service in a variety of ways so that you could also explain to your audience how they could make the most of it, what its benefits and drawbacks are, and so on. The more you know, the more your audience will trust you.

Most of the promotions you create are reviews in one way or another. And because of that, it's important that you also negatively review a product or service. Obviously, it's important to be honest, and don't always try to sugarcoat certain products or services. If they are not great, you may have to tell it like it is, or your audience will start to distrust you. However, only 5% to 10% of all the reviews you make should be negative since, at the end of the day, you still want to create content to promote and sell the services or products.

You'll have to build your SEO strategy before you create your content. Interesting content is not going to rank your content higher, but great content and a good SEO strategy certainly will. And for that, you need to do your keyword research. To optimize your content and use the right keywords, you can use several different tools to generate more traffic, such as Google Keyword Planner or Semrush. There are two main types of keywords that you should look into, regardless of the type of content you're producing. These are informal keywords that are introduced in your content and have the aim of informing your audience, and buyer-centric keywords that are there to help you convert those readers into buyers.

The length of your post should also be taken into consideration. Whether it's written or video content, the niche that you're targeting has a certain appropriate post length that usually works better with the audience you're targeting. The topics you're talking about are also relevant. But when we mention written text, small articles vary between 500 and 700 words, while longer articles can be between 1,500 and 2,500 words. Usually, when publishing smaller articles, you should do it every day or at least every other day. If you're publishing larger pieces of content, you should aim to publish between three and four times a month. This applies to video as well. Essentially, if you prefer to update your website, blog, or YouTube page, it's best to choose a shorter post length.

When creating good and informative content, you may opt to discuss things that matter to your audience. This is something that might seem obvious, but when actually done, many affiliate marketers fail to accomplish it. If you're promoting something that your audience is already familiar with, it's best to try and find information about it that is not in every other article online or that you've already mentioned before. If you're, for instance, writing a new blog post about a product that you've already talked about before, there needs to be something new for your audience; something that they haven't heard before about the product.

If you're discussing a brand-new product or service, try to be as detailed as possible (while still being engaging, of course). Your audience wants to know everything there is to know about this new product or service, from the way it works to the way it looks, and what problems it can solve. It's very common that a brand-new product has quite a few new features that you might want to talk about. If that's the case, don't talk about them all at once. Focus first on the ones that will influence your audience to make a purchase. You can make a second post or even a third one about all the other features later.

The tone of voice you use should appeal to the audience you're addressing, whether it's written or spoken content. While the age of your audience is important, such as using a conversational and friendly tone for younger people and a more formal tone for older people, so is the product or service you're discussing. Also, the words you use should also be relevant. Don't use terminology or jargon that you're not familiar with just to appear more knowledgeable about the topic. Chances are, your audience doesn't know those words either. And lastly, you should always strive for high-quality content. This is what will bring you people, whom you will ultimately convert into buyers. Make sure if you're writing your content, you use a grammar checker, and if you're speaking or recording your content, make sure you know how to pronounce the words properly and can make a concise and engaging speech.

Tools to Improve Your Content

While there are plenty of things that you can do to better promote your own content, there are two main things that really increase its exposure: email marketing and paid promotions.

Email marketing is something that you should try to build from the very beginning because it's one of the most efficient ways you can reach and expand your audience. It is especially fruitful when promoting content. The efficiency of email marketing is mostly due to the fact that people on that list have chosen to receive promotional emails from you, so they are willing to open the email and check what is inside to see whether something is relevant to them or not. However, building an email list takes time. The first thing you need to build in your email list is an email service provider or ESP. Besides allowing you to send emails, it also allows you to have subscribers and gives you many different types of reports and analytics (depending on the ESP you're using). While there are many ESPs, some of the main players in this industry are MailChimp (which allows you to have up to 1,000 subscribers with their free plan), ActiveCampaign, Campaign Monitor, ConvertKit, AWeber, and many others. It's important that you do your own research to find the one that suits your needs best. Make sure whatever email marketing strategy you use is directly linked to your overall marketing strategy. Some of the best methods to use with email marketing are to create awareness (whether it is brand awareness or product or service awareness) and conversion.

There are also three types of emails that you can send when promoting: communication emails, general campaigns and newsletters, and automated messaging. Communication via email should happen once your audience starts to grow. Their purpose is to choose segments of your audience (often based on demographics) to narrow your campaigns. When it comes to general campaigns and newsletter emails, these are usually sent to your whole email list and should be the most common type of email you send to your email list, especially at the beginning. Lastly, automated messaging emails that you send to anyone on your list that performs a certain action, such as welcoming emails for anyone signing up for your email list or when they purchase something from your own website (not through the affiliate link), etc.

Paid promotion, such as pay-per-click (PPC), can also help your content reach a wider audience. This is usually done through paid and targeted advertisements, and depending on where your audience is, you can run those ads there. Some of the most common examples of where these ads run are on social media platforms, retail websites, such as Amazon, or search engines, such as Google. The importance of creating a buyer's persona will certainly help you when you need to choose where to target your advertisement.

Tips on Creating Writing Content

Writing is one of the most used types of content, but because of that, to make it relevant in a sea of similar content, it has to be interesting and engaging to capture your audience's attention.

The very first thing you need to do, besides knowing what you're going to write about, is creating a compelling headline. Because of the usually small size of articles, everything you write should be relevant and engaging, so starting off with a compelling headline might get your audience hooked. When a headline is good, it provides essential information about the article, even for those who don't get past the headline and choose not to read the rest of the article. According to an analysis, 65 characters, or around 11 words, is the ideal length of a headline. However, the content of the headline is just as important. According to the same research, headlines that instruct the audience to do something are more likely to be shared on social media, especially when compared to other types of headlines. If your headline contains words or sentences such as "why you should know about..." or "why you need to know about..." you have greater chances of reaching a wider audience.

The introduction should be part of your written content, where you have an opportunity to get your readers hooked. While a great headline compels them to click on the article, a great intro persuades them to continue to read your article. Be wary of starting your introduction with topics adjacent to the main one; instead, you should go straight to what you've promised in the headline.

Writing for your audience is also quite important. This essentially means that instead of trying to please everyone, you should write for the niche you're growing. This has to be done from the headline until the last sentence of the article. However, the beginning is where you bring in the niche audience you are looking for. Try to be specific in your headline so that you can cater to the people who matter the most. Another thing that makes your content more compelling is to try to narrow the focus of your article. For example, if you're writing about social media marketing for retail companies, your title should be something like "How to Do Social Media Marketing for Retail Companies" instead of "How to Do Social Media Marketing for Small Businesses." Essentially, the broader the topic, the harder it is for you to write something interesting and valuable for your audience.

While you might already know this, being engaging is what makes your audience continue to grow and people continue to read your content. However, this is way easier said than done. An enticing headline and intro are without a doubt a great start, but you need to be engaging throughout the whole article. To do this, your information shouldn't be repetitive and boring. It should be something new that your audience has never heard before, which will be helpful to them. It's also about using simple language so the reader doesn't get tired faster. This often means shorter sentences and simpler words. However, don't oversimplify, or you might be underestimating your audience's intelligence.

Finding your voice—in this case, your unique brand voice—is crucial. This is how you speak to your audience, but also how compelling the storytelling of your articles is—the distinct personalities, the transparency, the memorable content, and other aspects. You should also plan your brand voice, even if it takes a little time to find it. When planning it, make sure you write down a description of your audience, your values and mission statement, examples of words or sentences that you'd like to use, and a description of your ideal relationship with the audience.

Within all of this, you also need to provide knowledge that your audience wants to read (this is also part of the engagement). For instance, if your article is about tips on how to look for a property, you can write about the current property market, the prices, and the trends, but if you don't offer tips, as you've promoted in your headline, or if those tips are generic and can be found in all the other articles on the search page, you are not providing knowledge that your audience wants to read. The best way to find out what your audience wants to read about is to check the data on all the tools that we've talked about.

While you might think that outlining is a waste of time, we can guarantee that it is not. It might take some of your time to create an outline for an article you're about to write, but it makes your writing a lot smoother and faster, and you'll end up with a more detailed and structured article. Outlining will also give you a better opportunity to add trust factors. Even in smaller niches, there are still many articles about the same topic as the one you're writing. Why would your audience choose your content instead of any other? This is where adding trust factors helps. It is essential to make your content trustworthy, and this can only happen if your audience knows that you do your research properly. You can link to studies, books, or other authoritative papers in your content so your audience knows that you've done proper research. Alternatively, you can also get those credible websites to link to your website, but this approach usually takes a little longer.

Tips on Creating Video Content

While writing is still the most popular way of creating content, video has been exponentially growing, and it might become the most used medium to create content soon. With the rapid increase in popularity of platforms such as YouTube and TikTok, video content is capturing the minds of the newer generation. So, how do you create great video content?

Planning

Much like any other form of content, you need planning. You can't simply hit the record button and come up with great content on the first take; there are many things that need to be thought out and properly planned. The first thing that you need to establish is your goal. What is it that you're aiming to accomplish with your video content? Once you've figured this out, you will be able to properly plan and shoot the video you want. It will be much easier to come up with engaging and informative things to say, and your thoughts will be more organized.

Identifying your target audience is a necessity. With all of the things you need to plan when starting your affiliate marketing career, identifying your target audience shouldn't be difficult at this point. However, sometimes it is good to remind yourself for whom you are making the content. Where you're going to post your content is also important, and sometimes it's not helpful to simply post it everywhere.

When you plan, you also need to do proper research on the topic you're going to talk about. Again, when choosing the right topic, you need to do some keyword searching if you want to rank as high as you possibly can on Google. When you're also doing videos, you should use YouTube by typing the main keyword into the search bar, and alternatives to that keyword will appear. This way, you can get a better idea of other related topics that you can pursue. Above all, just make sure you provide great content and knowledge to your audience, regardless of the topic you choose.

Choosing the right type of video is also important. If you regularly create video content, chances are that you prefer one or two types of videos (which also helps with brand recognition). However, we will give you some ideas on the main types of videos that are great for creating video content. The most popular are live-action and screen recording since they are a lot easier to create, but other options such as animation, motion graphics, or typography can also be great choices even if it takes more work to get them done. Whatever you choose, make sure the type of video suits the message you're trying to convey and matches your style and brand.

Writing a script falls under the category of planning. This is essentially the content that you will convey to your audience, so it's important that you think about it thoroughly. A script will tell you exactly what you need to say in an organized way, and it also makes it easier for you to lay any other images or videos on top if that's the type of video you are making. Scripting your video makes it easier to structure the story you're telling and also makes sure you don't forget essential bits of information. You can even do storyboards if that makes more sense to you, as long as everything is properly planned.

Most video content creators have a designated space where they always shoot their videos. This makes it easier for you to record the video and also adds a sense of familiarity to your audience, which gives more value to your brand. However, depending on the type of videos that you intend to do, changing your location might be essential, but it should only be done if it adds context to your content.

High-Quality Camera

Having the right camera can really make your content shine. Fortunately, with the advancement of technology, having a high-quality camera is not that expensive anymore. Here, you have two options: your camera phone (if you have a good phone) or a professional camera (which costs a little more).

If choosing a camera phone, make sure that when you purchase your phone, the quality is good (most of the latest iPhone and Samsung cameras can really do a great job). Essentially, look for 4K at 60 frames per second, which is comparable to most low-budget professional cameras. However, if you want to shoot high-quality video, a professional camera may be the best option (consider the type of content you want to shoot when deciding on a camera). Professional cameras also have more inbuilt features that phone cameras simply don't have, such as a swap lens feature, built-in image stabilization, or a wider palette of colors.

Lighting

Great lighting can really make a difference, especially if you don't want to spend too much on a professional camera. In fact, if your lighting is not great, most people will simply skip your videos. Now, there are two types of lighting: natural lighting and studio lighting. If you're just starting out and your location has great natural lighting, this should be enough to start shooting your videos. Shooting on cloudy days outside, for instance, can create really great lighting. If you shoot your videos indoors and it's hard to get natural lighting, you might want to invest in studio lighting instead.

Studio lighting gives you more versatility and allows you to shoot anywhere indoors. There are quite a few essential pieces of equipment when it comes to studio lighting, but knowing what you need the most is crucial so you don't spend all the money at once. Some of the things that you will want to add to your lighting equipment are, for instance, key and rim lights, reflectors, flashes, triggers, or shapers.

Audio

Audio is another area where you might need to invest quite some money, but it's not essential if you're just starting out. However, purchasing a cheap microphone from the start is crucial since built-in phone microphones are usually of worse quality than built-in cameras.

There are three main types of microphones that you should be looking at: dynamic, condenser, and lavalier microphones. Depending on the type of video and content you're shooting, they all have different applications.

Video Editing Software

Editing your videos is what makes mediocre content turn into great and engaging content. Even if the subject you're talking about is very interesting, if you publish it as is, chances are that your audience won't be as engaged. You need to use video editing software to color grade, add titles and subtitles, add transitions, tweak audio and visual components, and add special effects that make your video content look more professional.

In this area, you have plenty of choices, some free and others paid, but if you're just starting out, we recommend that you get your hands on a free video editing program and then invest in a more professional program once you know what you're doing.

Video Composition

Framing your video can make it look a lot better, so take some time to understand the different frames there are and how you can improve your video content. One of the most popular framing techniques is the "rule of thirds," where you essentially divide the frame into 3 × 3 grids so you know where you should be positioned as well as any other objects on camera. There are other framing techniques that might be relevant for you, such as leading lines, symmetry, or framing within your frame.

Learn How to Be Comfortable on Camera

This might not be relevant for all types of video content, but if you or any other person is going to appear on camera, you need to make sure they are comfortable doing it. Camera presence, as it is called, can make your videos easier to watch and convey confidence, which is especially relevant if you're promoting products or services.

There are many techniques and exercises that you can try out to make this seem more natural to you, such as standing up or sitting straight, having your shoulders back, and looking focused. The way you speak is also relevant, and here you should aim to speak clearly and slowly while pronouncing every word properly.

Being at ease in front of the camera is one of those things that improves with practice, so the best thing to do is shoot as many videos as possible.

Filming in Small Segments

Shooting small parts of the video at a time is a great way to make your video content better. This is because it is easier to edit, and you can shoot several takes and pick the best ones. You will also remain more focused throughout several segments instead of trying to shoot the video all at once.

Get Clicks to Your Links

While great content is certainly a good way to get clicks on your links and eventually sell the products or services you're promoting, there are other things to consider if you want to improve the number of people that click on your links. We've seen that techniques to increase traffic, such as paid promotion, can work well, but there are things that you can do without investing more money.

Proper link placement is perhaps the best way to get more clicks on your links. It's not just adding links to your content and hoping for the best. Most seasoned affiliate marketers know exactly where they should place their links in their content.

The best place to add links is at the top of the article (if it's written content, of course). Usually, the introduction is a great place to add links (and, more importantly, the most relevant links) because the majority of people will not read the whole article. As you might know, people have a much shorter attention span nowadays, so the higher you place your link, the more chances you have that they will click on it.

Using longer anchor text is also a good idea if you want to increase the click rate on your links. Previously, anchor text was much shorter and usually only focused on keywords; however, due to the extensive use of anchor text, longer forms can be more effective. An anchor text is the clickable text of a link that is frequently highlighted in a different color. When adding longer anchor text, ensure that it can be done in an actionable way and that it makes sense in the context of what you're writing, as well as be accurate once the readers click on the link. However, don't think that the more links you use, the better your chances are of getting more clicks. Overuse of links can actually make your content less coherent, and it will simply look worse. There's no ideal number for the number of links that you add to your article, but an average of 10 (also depending on the size of the article) is usually a good amount.

One of the most underutilized techniques when it comes to getting clicks on your links is to minimize distractions. We've already said that, in general, people have a much shorter attention span, so trying to minimize distractions in your posts can go a long way to keeping your audience focused on what you're trying to accomplish. Less distraction often means less advertising, fewer images, or fewer sidebar links. You certainly can (and should) have these elements, but too many of them will simply distract your readers from your content.

While there's value in quality content, it is important that you know how to control your audience's attention and keep the focus on what really matters to you. However, you should aim to reach great content quality and user-friendly posts.

Writing a blog makes it easier to add affiliate marketing links, but there are other platforms where that might be a little harder to understand, albeit not impossible. For instance, how do you attach affiliate links if you do video content on YouTube? Or use other platforms, such as Facebook? Let's take a look.

On YouTube, for instance, there are two main ways you can incorporate affiliate links. You can do it through reviews or vlogs. In both of these cases, you should attach the affiliate link in the description below the video. On a social media page such as Facebook, you can post something advertising a product or service with a link attached to it, or alternatively, you can also use Facebook advertising to target certain groups.

Instagram, on the other hand, is a very different type of social media platform that is based on images. So, if you want to add an affiliate link, you can do so by using the description box or tagging the image with the affiliate link.

Converting Clicks Into Sales

Getting traffic and clicks is a good start but that won't matter in the long run if you can't convert those clicks into sales. It's the same as having many people visit your brick-and-mortar shop without purchasing anything. So, what can you do to convert that traffic and clicks into actual sales?

While there's not a single method to do this, there are several things that you can do to make your conversion rate higher. However, it's important to note that sometimes the merchant's website can also be at fault, and it's not entirely your lack of knowledge or appropriate techniques. As you grow as an affiliate marketer, you will be more "picky" when it comes to the brands that you work for.

Attracting the right traffic is one of the first things you should aim to do. The most common issue with affiliate marketers who face this problem is that they might be marketing to the wrong crowd. If you're selling women's shoes and all you target is middle-aged men, then there's your issue. This doesn't mean you won't sell anything, but you're not getting the most out of your marketing strategies.

Another common problem is that your audience can't find what they want fast enough. We've mentioned the current attention span of most people online, and this is what we are referring to. If they can't find their answer or the product or service they are looking for in less than 30 seconds, chances are they will move on to other things. You need to give them reasons to stick around and engage them from the start.

It's enough that many merchant websites have too many pop-ups that make anyone visiting want to leave. While there's nothing you can do about their website, you can reduce your pop-ups on your own website (this only affects websites and blogs, not social media accounts). While showing pop-ups might be essential for you, you can make them less annoying by only showing one at a time or restricting them to one or maybe two different pages. You can use slide-ins for pop-ups instead of just having the pop-ups pop onto the screen. These are far less intrusive and, as a result, a lot less infuriating for the user. They also follow the screen even if they scroll up or down, making it a better promotional tool. Another type of pop-up that works well is the floating bar. They usually appear at the top of the page, and much like slide-ins, they stick to the user's screen and are less intrusive.

It can also happen that your website is hard to navigate, and, as we've said before, if your audience has a short attention span, they will immediately leave your page if they can't immediately find what they want. There are several things that can make a page hard to navigate, such as outdated design, slow loading, or random text and images all over the page.

Making your website trustworthy is an excellent way to convert clicks into sales. You wouldn't purchase something from a dubious promotional website, would you? Who's to tell if the link you added directs to the official webpage of the brand? So, how do you make it more trustworthy? There are a number of things that you can do. You can make sure there are no grammar issues and that your customer testimonials are real, try to rank higher on Google searches, or use trustworthy backlinks.

If you accept reviews from members of your audience, make sure you make them visible and take them seriously (especially the bad reviews). The same goes for any testimonials that you want to add.

Great link placement is important, and strategically placing a Call To Action (CTA) can make a world of difference when it comes to converting clicks into sales. Besides creating engaging CTAs, you need to know where they are most effective within your content. This is especially true if you use CTA buttons that redirect users to the merchant pages. Some of the best places to add your CTAs and CTA buttons are above the fold or in sidebars.

Calling the attention of exiting users is also a good way to try and convert more sales. As we've talked about, there are many reasons why someone would leave your website, such as the fact that they couldn't find what they wanted or too many intrusive pop-ups. There's another pop-up that can help you capture those exiting users called "exit-intent pop-ups." Usually, when a user wants to exit your website, these appear automatically and encourage them to stay by offering promotions or signing up for your email list.

You can also track your conversions with some of the tools that we've already talked about to identify what the problem is. Google Analytics, for instance, is a great choice to try and understand what your conversions look like. However, when trying out some of these methods, it is important that you test them and find out which ones work best for you (this is also where analyzing your data comes in handy). You can run A/B tests and try different approaches to understand which methods are working and which aren't. Even if these take some time, they will make it more efficient in the long run.

In the following chapter, we will talk about what type of affiliate marketer you intend to be.

Checklist

	Research different affiliate programs
	Decide on the right affiliate program for you
	Decide on an affiliate product you want to start with
	Plan what content will work with the niche and product you chose
	Create a plan on how to generate click and how to convert them to sales

Chapter 3:

What Type of Affiliate Marketer Do You Want to Be?

Now that you know the basics of affiliate marketing, you might be wondering how many types of marketers there are. Well, there are quite a few, and there's certainly one type that you will enjoy being.

The different types of affiliate marketers are intrinsically related to the type of items that you sell, whether they are physical products or services. We will investigate all of the major types and how to promote them. We will also touch on the essential skills that will help to identify what type of affiliate marketer you are.

The last part of this chapter is dedicated to successful stories, and this is not only to give you the confidence you might need but also to show you that successful affiliate marketers can come from anywhere and start their adventure in the most varied branches of the industry.

The Main Types of Affiliate Marketing

We've been talking about affiliate marketing and how it works, but to have a full understanding of what affiliate marketing is, you need to know the three main categories. These are: unattached affiliate marketing, related affiliate marketing, and involved affiliate marketing. If this means nothing to you, don't worry; we will explain everything you need to know. In fact, we have been talking about all of them to this point, although we haven't given them proper names.

Unattached Affiliate Marketing

Unattached affiliate marketing is one of the most common types of affiliate marketing. Essentially, these are based on pay-per-click campaigns, and there's no link between you (the affiliate marketer) and the customer or consumer. This is usually called "no presence, no authority in the niche." So, what is required of you is to simply place an affiliate link in front of the consumer. This is one of the most common types of affiliate marketing because you don't need to grow and nurture an audience; you don't even need your own website to do this. However, many dedicated affiliate marketers frown upon this type of affiliate marketing model because it's essentially an income-generating model and requires no work on your behalf. It's also far more difficult to make a decent income if you don't have an audience and are just targeting random people online.

Related Affiliate Marketing

Related affiliate marketing is a little closer in terms of your online presence with your audience. In this type of affiliate marketing, you can use mediums such as blogs, videos, podcasts, or social media accounts, although you're not necessarily using any of the products or services that you advertise, and the niche is only somehow related. So, if you have a financial blog, your promotion might be anything that is related to finance but not necessarily any specific product or service that you talk about in your blog.

However, even if not directly related, there are more chances for you to make a decent income through affiliate marketing. Usually, these affiliate links are not in your text (if you're using a written medium), and they appear on sidebars, banners, or any other place but in your text. Here you have a little more authority, so you can choose where you should place your links.

Involved Affiliate Marketing

If you promote a product or service that you use and believe to be true, then that's called involved affiliate marketing. For many marketers out there, this is the best way to approach affiliate marketing since you're recommending the product or service directly to your audience. Unlike other types of marketing, you are promoting this in your content, so if you're using blogging, for instance, you're linking to the merchant's page directly in your text. For this type of marketing to work, it's best that you actually use the promoted product or service so you can be true to your recommendation (although this is not always the case). However, your audience believes in you, and in a way, it's your name and reputation on the line if you promote something directly and it ends up being a bad product or a bad service. You can see it is using your reputation to promote something instead of using your money (such as PPC-type affiliate marketing). In this type of affiliate marketing, you also have full authority to promote and place the affiliate link on your website.

It's not always easy to start off with involved affiliate marketing, and for you to have the time to build trust and an audience, you might have to start with other forms of affiliate marketing, but your goal should always be to follow involved affiliate marketing.

Best Mediums for Affiliate Marketing

We've already mentioned a few platforms where affiliate marketing performs well, but all of that depends on your skills as well as the medium and products you want to use. Here, we will go through some affiliate marketing mediums to find out what products and services work best in each of them.

Influencer and Social Media Affiliate Marketing

Influencers have emerged as a critical component of social media. These are people with huge followings on their social media pages, which allows them to leverage that presence to promote products and services to their audiences.

To be an influencer affiliate marketer, you have to spend time and effort building your audience by creating engaging content so brands can approach you and offer to have you promote their products. For brands, influencer affiliate marketing is one of the most trustworthy ways of creating genuine leads and sales, expanding their brand awareness, and creating great content.

At the end of the day, this is just another marketing strategy that yields high profits if done properly. For that to happen, you need to cooperate with brands that fit in with your persona and that "make sense."

In theory, an influencer affiliate marketing strategy can promote anything, depending on the type of influencer you are. If you are a beauty type or fashion influencer, you can promote makeup products or clothes; if you're a sports person, you can promote any type of sports outfit or energy drinks, etc. So, pretty much anything as long as you shape and market yourself as the type of influencer you want to be.

Blogging and Affiliate Marketing

Affiliate marketing through blogging is one of the most common and profitable ways to enter the affiliate marketing industry. We've talked extensively about blogging and affiliate marketing, so we won't go into detail here, but the most important thing is to join an affiliate program and promote the products or services through your written content. What is important here is understanding the best types of affiliate programs for bloggers.

We've previously mentioned some affiliate programs such as Rakuten Marketing and CJ Affiliate, which are great choices to join if you're a blogger. Now, there are others.

For instance, ShareASale is an affiliate program with many different merchants and great pay. Although they don't offer too many popular brands, this can be a great place for beginners to start. However, one of the best features of this affiliate program is its search filters, which allow you to filter your results in many different ways, including by commission.

Creative Market is another excellent affiliate program that is far more niched than the ones we've mentioned before. It focuses on photos and graphics, as well as themes for WordPress. If this is your type of audience or in line with the products and services that you want to offer, it's certainly a great choice. Other websites with great affiliate programs for bloggers include Coursera, HubSpot, and ConvertKit.

A great way to become better at affiliate marketing through blogging is to simply visit successful affiliate marketing blogs. We will give you some of the top ones in the industry for you to have a look at and learn as much as you can about the most varied topics.

For example, the John Chow blog covers a wide range of topics, from food to travel to technology. They usually use two forms of content: written and video.

Mobile Affiliate Marketing

Mobile affiliate marketing is one of the newest types of affiliate marketing, and it consists of driving sales or traffic to the merchant's website through mobile devices. It's important to make a distinction because there are many affiliate programs that cater to mobile marketing. Apart from that, there aren't many differences between it and other affiliate programs.

One of the advantages this type of affiliate marketing has, is that the content and promotions are more engaging because that's the nature of mobile devices. With this, you are capable of reaching people a lot easier, which is making more and more businesses turn to this type of affiliate marketing. Essentially, with all of the features designed to be performed on mobile devices, you don't need a laptop or a computer because everything, including tracking tools and other features, works from your mobile.

When it comes to choosing the best affiliate marketing program, you need to do your research. As you now know, different affiliate programs (even mobile ones) work better in some businesses than others. When choosing what mobile affiliate marketing program to use, it is also relevant that you know which platform your audience spends their time on.

Coupon Affiliate Programs

A coupon affiliate marketer is a person who promotes coupon affiliate offers using coupon affiliate programs. These types of programs usually offer great commissions as well as great conversion rates. In fact, most of the time, the marketer gets a commission simply by driving traffic to the merchant's website without the need for a sale. In every other way, these affiliate programs function exactly like any other program in the industry.

There are quite a few coupon affiliate programs, such as Coupons.com, Local Flavor, Deal Taker, Honey.com, WikiBuy, Advanced Coupons, Top Cashback, or Ibotta.

For example, Coupons.com is one of the largest in the niche and offers a wide selection of both printable and digital promo codes and coupons. The best part is that their offers cover a large variety of other niches, such as office products, clothes, pet food, and so on. Another advantage of this website's program, in particular, is that they have top-tier brands as partners.

Top Cashback, for example, works a little differently when it comes to the end consumer, and instead of coupons, they offer cashback at more than 4,000 online retailers. You will have to do your own research to find out what program is best for you, but the type of affiliate marketing that you should expect to perform is a mix of unattached and related affiliate marketing.

Affiliate Email Marketing

This is another type of medium for affiliate marketing that we've briefly talked about before. This sort of approach derives from classic email marketing, but instead of promoting your own services and products, you are promoting the merchant's.

Much like traditional email marketing, these emails are written and designed to gather as many subscribers as possible, but in this case, the end game is to convert and drive traffic to the merchant's websites. Because of the nature of affiliate email marketing, this is a great way to increase conversions since they cater to a very accurate audience with engaging content.

When looking for an affiliate email marketing program, make sure it has a good reputation and is established in the industry. You should also ensure that your niche matches the niches of the program and that it has a good conversion rate. Besides that, you need to do some research and try to understand if they offer the basic features, such as tracking engagement, sales conversion and budget tracking, as well as performance-related insights and recommendations.

Some of the best affiliate email marketing programs out there include ConvertKit (which we've already mentioned), HubSpot, and Omnisend.

Affiliate Marketing Incentive Programs (Loyalty Programs)

Some affiliate programs offer incentives to high-performing marketers who reach certain goals. This could range from more money to other offers. This is essentially a tactic from the affiliate programs to incentivize their marketers to continue their good performance.

Affiliate programs know that it's hard to come across hard-working marketers that enjoy what they do and do it well. In order to keep those high-performing affiliate marketers, they are able to offer compensation.

If you work with such an affiliate program, incentives come in many different forms. Increased commissions are perhaps the most common, and most of the time they work as a tiered commission that goes up from time to time. For instance, if you reach your goal every quarter, then your commission will increase. Sometimes your commission goes up according to your sales increase from previous months or quarters. So, for example, if your sales go up 15%, you might have an increased commission of 5%.

Another way of rewarding affiliate marketers is through offers and deals. This usually comes in the form of discounts on products or services the affiliate program works with. Another popular way is to receive gift cards from top-tier brands. Merchandise, free gifts, or samples are yet another way some affiliate programs like to compensate their marketers. All of this might come directly from the brands the affiliate program works with, or it could be an initiative from the affiliate program itself.

Recently, a popular way to reward affiliate marketers is through gamification, or in this case, sales gamification. Essentially, brands or affiliate programs turn tasks and goals into achievements that, once reached, reward the marketer. Streak bonuses are quite popular, for instance, if you, as a marketer, manage to convert four or five sales within a week. Another great way is to create a leaderboard where marketers can see their ranking. In the same line of thinking, leveling up is becoming quite popular too. This is a tactic used by some brands and affiliate programs to bring their marketers closer to the company's goal. And so, the program's success is also your success. Usually, marketers are a lot more involved in the program's or brand's goal, and because of that, this method is often used in smaller affiliate programs or smaller brands.

There's another simple way affiliate programs can incentivize marketers, and that's through updates, guides, and new information. As you reach your goals, the program offers you more information and allows you to become more involved in the program itself. You can give feedback on how to improve the platform and bring in new ideas, etc. This brings a good sense of responsibility, and being involved in a company makes you care more and achieve better results. Some of the affiliate programs that we've mentioned previously offer these incentives. So, when you're searching for affiliate programs, make sure they have this feature.

News Websites and Review Websites

News websites can be a great way to promote products and some affiliate programs allow you access to them. However, this is hard when you're starting out and don't have a name in the industry. The same is true for review websites; while they might have a lot of organic traffic, you can only get access to those programs if you've built your career around that type of medium. In either case, these are great mediums with a lot of exposure, which will certainly provide a lot of exposure to the products or services advertised.

What Type of Affiliate Marketer Do You Want to Be?

Some types of affiliate marketing do require a specific skill set, and most of them have quite broad skills that you need to have or work on if you want to succeed. For example, if you want to do influencer affiliate marketing, besides being savvy with social media platforms and being able to gather an audience, you are also required to perform well on camera and have great communication skills to put together engaging videos. While, if you're a blog affiliate, you're required to have great writing skills to write about things and persuade people to purchase them. If you focus solely on mobile affiliate marketing, then it'll be beneficial to have great knowledge of all the software available to you on mobile. If you are an email marketing affiliate, then engaging people in your content in a small space such as an email requires a good balance of conversational yet persuasive writing skills.

However, there are a few skills that you need to succeed in the affiliate marketing industry, regardless of the type of work you do. For example, a good knowledge of web design can go a long way. If you don't have that knowledge, then every time you want to change your website, you will have to hire a web designer, which can eat quite a bit of your profit. While you can start with a template website like WordPress, as your business grows, you may want to upgrade to a more professional-looking website.

Problem solving should come naturally to you and you should be confident in decision-making to succeed as an affiliate marketer. Problems will certainly come your way in this line of work, and because you are in it on your own, you won't be able to rely on anyone. With this, you will have to make decisions on your own, even though you have tools that can assist you.

Creativity is another skill that is quite valuable in many different industries, and affiliate marketing is no exception. You will need something that makes you stand out from the crowd, and many times, it's that creativity in the way you create your content or build your marketing strategies that makes the difference. Creativity is also excellent to have if you're trying to create and establish a brand. It will allow you to develop and establish your vision a lot faster and draw people in.

You will analyze a lot of data in this line of work, so understanding how to read the data you are presented can be crucial. A big part of being an affiliate marketer is to look at data and try to understand where you can perform better and market your website and your merchant's products or services better. You will also analyze data to know what type of audience you're looking for and where you can find them.

An essential skill to have is marketing and sales. At the end of the day, you need to be able to sell a certain service or product to someone to make a profit, so having this type of skill is crucial for your success.

Success Tips

One of the tips other successful affiliate marketers share is to focus on your conversions and not on your commissions. Essentially, you shouldn't be chasing the high commission rate but instead focus on promoting the brands that give you higher conversion rates, which is far more efficient. Look at these two scenarios: there's a brand that pays $1,500 per sale, but their conversion rate is only around 0.05%, and then you have another affiliate program that pays you $2 in commission, and their conversion is about 25%. It's far better to have consistent and almost certain commissions while growing your audience than to have a big payout that happens twice a year, if at all. If you have lower commissions but get paid more frequently, your audience will start to trust you, and other brands will also approach you.

Another tip that most of these successful affiliate marketers share is to build a subscriber list as soon as you can. This is the only way you can build your brand and gather a sizable audience. Most also advise creating incentives for people to subscribe to your email subscription, such as deals and other rewards. This way, you can also track how fast you're growing and understand what is working and what you have to change in order to keep expanding. You will need to use some of the tools that we've already mentioned to be able to track this properly.

One important tip, and perhaps the most important of all, is to follow the rules. It's important to understand that the brands you're promoting have put a lot of effort into expanding their brand and promoting their products or services. So, whether you make reviews or any other promotional content, it's important that you don't claim things that are not true about the brand or use their trademarks to build something on your behalf. Most of the time, the brand in question will realize this and penalize you, which makes your followers not trust you.

Being successful in the affiliate marketing business is not something that happens overnight. It requires time and effort, and because of that, if you're getting into the game, you should commit to the long haul. Consistency is perhaps the best way to describe what it takes to succeed. At the end of the day, it's a business, and business takes some time to bring profits. You need to be able to constantly grow your audience, so your chances of profiting increase. Begin small, learn about your audience, and discover what motivates them. High-quality content is also something that might take some time for you to hone properly, but it will help as long as you're persistent and don't expect quick results.

Diversifying your affiliate partners is also a good way to make sure you have results. This comes from the saying, "Don't put all your eggs in one basket." The reason for this in affiliate marketing is that companies can simply close their affiliate program or cut their commissions. A good rule to follow is to not have more than 50% of your commission revenue come from a single affiliate program. Also, when launching a new website, make sure you have content there first before you apply for an affiliate program. You can't expect to promote products or services if there's nothing there in terms of content. No one is going to visit your website if there's nothing interesting for them to read or see. There's no rule when it comes to the amount of content that you should have, but anything between 15 and 20 pieces of content should be a good starting point. Also, keep in mind that the higher the quality of the content, the more likely it is to drive more traffic to your website.

While keyword competition and monthly search volume are great metrics to track, one that many beginners seem to overlook is search intent. It simply refers to what your target audience is looking for. Is it to seek information? Is it to purchase something? Or simply to be entertained? You need to look at what your audience is looking for so you can provide them with exactly what they want. This will drive traffic to your website, which will eventually lead to sales and commissions. Also, don't ignore shopping seasons. We know there's a lot of competition during those times, but you should make an effort to put out more promotions and advertising during those times because the demand is also greater. However, not only are Black Friday, Cyber Monday, and Christmas great shopping seasons; make an extra effort during Valentine's Day, Father's Day, and Mother's Day as well. If you do this, you're not only increasing your chances of making more sales, but you're also increasing your chances of growing your audience.

In the next chapter, we will go through some of the less fun but essential information when it comes to the business of affiliate marketing: taxes. This is a fundamental part of any business, and it's crucial that you understand how to pay and report your taxes. We will talk about the different taxes that an affiliate marketer might have to pay, what tax forms to file, and regulations in and outside of the US.

Checklist

	Decide what type of affiliate marketing will work for you
	Decide what medium would work best for your type of affiliate marketing

Chapter 4:

Affiliate Marketers and Taxes

Taxes, particularly in the affiliate marketing industry, are a bit of a gray area that can cause a lot of stress for new affiliate marketers. In this chapter, we will help you navigate this topic so you can have the necessary knowledge to get this done properly.

We will start with the types of taxes that affiliate marketers have to pay and when they have to pay them, then we will move on to the different forms out there and explain which ones might better suit you and your business. Besides the US, we will also discuss what you have to do if you're an affiliate marketer that is located in another country, such as the UK, Germany, or Australia. Lastly, we will also discuss other things that you will need to consider when filing and paying your taxes, such as tracking them, what tax deductions are, and how to apply them in your tax return.

What Taxes Do Affiliate Marketers Pay?

As an affiliate marketer, you pay taxes as a self-employed worker, and so you have to pay for social security as well as Medicare. This comes with a roughly 15% tax. Not only that, but there are times that you might have to create estimates about your affiliate marketing payments for both federal and state income taxes to be paid to the IRS.

In the US, because you're selling the services or products that you are promoting, you won't have to pay sales taxes, which is one of the most common questions newcomers have. Only the brand or company that actually sells the services or products has to pay sales taxes. However, it's crucial that, even with the information we will give you here, you still talk with an accountant because tax rates vary in every state and country.

However, affiliate marketing profits are only taxable if you make more than $600. Anything below that figure is not taxable, but you still have to file your tax return. While filing your taxes might sound complicated, you should not neglect them because the IRS will eventually find out, and you will have to pay fines on top of what you already owe them.

The Different Tax Forms

While there are numerous forms to pay taxes, as an affiliate marketer, you really only have to know about two: the Schedule C and the Schedule SE tax forms.

The Schedule C, or Form 1040, is for sole proprietors to report their profit and loss. Essentially, you will have to report any profit or loss as well as other general information regarding your business. While there are services that can help you with filing it and an accountant to guide you, we will leave a link from the IRS website that gives you detailed information about filing this form.

- www.irs.gov/instructions/i1040sc

The Schedule SE, also from the Form 1040, is for self-employed people. This form is used to figure out any tax due from your self-employed business. It is also linked to the Social Security Administration to find out if you are entitled to benefits, both from social security and Medicare. Here's the link for the instructions on how to file the form:

- www.irs.gov/instructions/i1040sse

The main difference here is that Schedule C has to be filed if you're registered as a sole proprietor, and Schedule SE has to be filed if you're only self-employed.

Tracing Your Taxable Income

It's important that you track your income through affiliate marketing, and it's certainly something that you should actively do because it makes it a lot easier when it's time for you to file your taxes.

However, while at the beginning it's quite simple, once you start growing, it becomes a little harder for you to track it. This is where specialized software that helps you track your income comes in handy. QuickBooks or FreshBooks, for example, not only help you track your income from affiliate marketing, but they also help you file your taxes and send them to the IRS. At the beginning, you can simply track this with a spreadsheet, but get used to using a specialized program as soon as your income and expenses start to grow.

Tax Deductions for Affiliate Marketers

Essentially, any deduction related to the practice of affiliate marketing can be considered a tax deduction. This can be a lengthy list of things such as your website maintenance, subscriptions, any employees that you might have, marketing promotion for your website, your phone bill if you use it for your profession, and if you conduct your business at home, you can even claim energy and water bills. However, it's always best for you to bring in an accountant to make sure those things do qualify. Anything that qualifies as a personal expense cannot be claimed as a tax deduction.

When filing your taxes, it is best to keep any receipts from your expenses and give them to your accountant if you have one since oftentimes the IRS might need proof of these expenses.

Tax Regulations Outside of the United States

If you live outside of the United States, the procedure is the same because you must always register as self-employed; however, there are a few differences when it comes to filing your taxes and which forms to use.

Filing Taxes in the United Kingdom

It's fairly easy to register as self-employed in the UK by visiting www.gov.uk/register-for-self-assessment and following the necessary steps. First, you need to get a government gateway login, which can also be acquired on the UK government website, then register for self-assessment and, finally, as a self-employed person. The website above is very comprehensive and easy to follow. By following the steps they indicate, you will easily be able to get everything in order. You will need to have a National Insurance Number (NIN) and be a resident of the country.

To get your government gateway, simply follow the steps on this website: www.gov.uk/log-in-register-hmrc-online-services/register. To pay your taxes, you will need to visit the government website and file the SA100 form. As an affiliate marketer, you're not a company, so you can simply fill this form and send it to HMRC.

Filing Taxes in Germany

To register as a self-employed person in Germany, nationality in either Germany or any other country in the EU is required. If you don't have that, you will first have to get a residency permit. After you've done that, you will have to file a form called the *Fragenbogen zur steuerlichen Erfassung* to file your taxes. This form has to be sent to your regional or local tax office. However, doing this online is far easier than going to the government website: www.formulare-bfinv.de/ffw/content.do. Because this form is only in German, it would be helpful to know German or enlist some help to complete and file it. Getting a tax advisor or an accountant can be quite helpful.

Filing Taxes in Australia

In order to be self-employed in Australia, you have to register for an Australia Business Number (ABN). To first do that, you need to go to the Australian Business Register. All you have to do is go to this website and follow the steps there. It's a very simple process: www.abr.gov.au/business-super-funds-charities/applying-abn.

You either need an Australian citizenship or a residence permit in the country. When registering, you will have to give details about your business, your tax number, as well as more general things such as your address and phone number.

To file taxes as a self-employed person, you will have to file the "Tax File Number—Application for Individuals," which is Form NAT 1432. However, you first need to apply for a tax file number (TFN). You can do this online by following this website:

identityservice.auspost.com.au/ato/landing.

You will also have to book an interview within 30 days of completing the form, where you will have to present identification documents.

Filing Taxes in Russia

If you don't hold Russian citizenship, you will have to apply for one or acquire a residence permit as well as open a bank account before you can register as self-employed and file taxes. To register, you need to file Form R21002 for individuals and have any legal identification documents if you're not of Russian citizenship, as well as residency. You will also have to show documents proving that you're not a convicted felon, certified by a notary. Because the Form R21002 is only in Russian, you either have to know how to speak the language or get someone to translate it for you.

After that, using your address in the country, you need to register with your local tax office. You can do it online through the website of the municipality or city, so there's not a single website that you have to go to.

In the next chapter, we will talk about the many affiliate marketing strategies that can help you start your business in the strongest way possible. Besides talking about the different strategies available to you from the very start, we will also give you some of the best tips when you're just starting out.

Checklist

	Do research about tax requirements in your region
	Find all of the different tax forms you will need
	Download a tool to track your affiliate marketing income

Chapter 5:

Strategies to Kickstart Your Affiliate Marketing

In the next chapter, we will talk about the many affiliate marketing strategies that can help you start your business in the strongest way possible. Besides talking about the different strategies available to you from the very start, we will also give you some of the best tips when you're just starting out.

You've now acquired some good knowledge about how affiliate marketing works and the things that you need to do to get all set up. We will now discuss some beginner's strategies to get you started. It's important that you understand and practice these strategies to get used to what it is to be an affiliate marketer, so you can then grow your business and try more advanced methods.

Before we start, it is important to make a distinction between products that you might promote and services that you might work with as an affiliate marketer.

Physical products are the most common items to promote, mostly because of Amazon and its extremely popular affiliate marketing program and because they are the easiest to purchase in terms of use. Even though physical products are not the ones that bear more fruit when it comes to profits and commissions. While Amazon offers lower commissions, there are other brands that offer slightly higher ones, but in general, it is harder to make a sale.

Information products can be anything from a course to any other digital product that contains information. These tend to cost more and, because of that, offer higher commissions. These information products are also quite easy to promote because, through information, they usually provide a solution to a problem. Although the brands that offer programs with these products are more spread out and smaller in size, you'll have to do a little more research to find the ideal product and program. For instance, one of the largest affiliate programs for information products is Coursera.

Service products are essentially services and are the other large type of promotional item in the affiliate marketing business after physical products. These are also very diverse, from themes in WordPress to any type of software. You will have to conduct proper research and find a service that you're passionate about and that you will be happy to promote, as well as one that yields great profit. While harder to sell than physical products, service products have higher commissions, usually between 15% and 30%.

Beginner Strategies

A great strategy depends on a number of factors: your products and/or services, the platform(s) you use to promote them, your scalability and the targets you wish to reach, both in audience and sales. We will name some of the best strategies to start your affiliate marketing career so that you can understand where you stand within these parameters. This will ensure that you take advantage of the best strategy for you.

Shop Around for Best Commission Rates

You will have to do a little digging to find the best commission rates within your niche, but it's certainly worth it. You will work smarter instead of harder if you do this. While you may be misled by what appear to be high commissions at first, never settle for the highest commissions you find at any time. Rates change all the time in different affiliate programs, so make it a habit to browse around for new commission rates or even new affiliate programs that might be paying higher.

Build Connections With Your Audience and Community

We've talked extensively about finding your own niche and audience, and while that's not an easy task in itself, building a connection with them is certainly the ultimate goal. This, however, can take quite some time, but your conversion will certainly increase. While affiliate marketing tools can also increase sales, having your own connection with your community is far more valuable.

Find a Mentor

There are things that only come with experience, no matter how much time you put into your affiliate marketing career at the beginning. And so, getting someone with experience in the field to guide you is one of the most valuable things you can do. A mentor can help you avoid losing money or even an audience, and in order to make your affiliate marketing career profitable, you can't afford to lose those at any cost, or it will just take longer for you to get back on top. A mentor can also vet all of your strategies and pinpoint all the ones that will actually make a difference in your affiliate marketing career. Besides saving money and potential members of your audience, you will also save a lot of time.

Diversify Your Affiliate Programs

Diversification can give you leverage and allow you more freedom to make a good profit even if one of your programs goes a little slow. As we've said before, companies can simply close their programs, so make sure you find at least a handful of them so you have a safety net.

Get Creative Promoting Products

Affiliate marketing has fierce competition, so the more creatively you promote your products or services, the more you will be able to convert and sell. You have a lot of room for creativity when it comes to promoting; you can choose your posts and use your affiliate links regardless of the medium you use (or even use several mediums to create something unique).

Check out the top affiliate marketers to see how they promote their products and add a little bit of yourself to everything you do. This is a bulletproof way of not only connecting with your audience but also selling more.

Start Partnerships Directly With Brands

You can cut out the middleman (in this case, affiliate programs) and work directly with brands. When you are at the beginning of your affiliate marketing career, this might not be the easiest thing. As your audience grows, you can start asking about brands that you've been promoting through affiliate programs.

This way, you can earn much larger commissions and have more control over the things you promote and how you promote them. While being an affiliate marketer influencer makes this far easier, you can still do it through all other channels. If, for instance, your blog becomes quite popular, you will have a lot more exposure, and brands will certainly hire you to promote their products or services directly. It is best to start with smaller brands and work your way up from there. Also, make sure you work on your negotiating skills since you will be the one negotiating your commissions.

Add Affiliate Links Where Most Traffic Is Located

There's no need for you to create new content to increase your profit from your affiliate links. Simply go through your existing content and look for the most popular pieces (traffic-wise). Use some of the tools that we've mentioned before to help you out. Once you know which ones generate more traffic, you can add affiliate links to them. Then, promote every single page with the new affiliate link using paid promotions or any other technique you might want to use.

However, you don't want to pick pages that are already making great sales; you want to pick the ones with more traffic that are not doing so well when it comes to conversions, or you might mess with the pages that are bringing you profit.

Customize Links for Different Countries

If you have an audience from many different countries, you might want to customize it to that specific country. This is because it can be quite annoying for members of your audience to click on the link and see the message, "This content is not available in your country." Or finding out shipping fees are incredibly high because they are on the wrong country's website. This is a sure way to lose your audience. To give you an example, if you're an Amazon affiliate, you might want to use a tool called Amazon OneLink, which allows overseas users to click on it and be taken to the Amazon page for their country. However, there are many other software programs that can be used to change that. Just search for geo-targeting (or geo-tagging) and research the programs that work best for you.

Marketing for Free

While sometimes you might want to put some money aside for paid promotions, you should be able to maximize your opportunities to profit by doing affiliate marketing for free. This doesn't mean you will work for free; instead, use any free tool and medium you can to promote your products or services. This is particularly great at the beginning of your career as an affiliate marketer because you won't have to pay for ads or web hosting this way.

For example, email marketing is a great way to promote products for free. Yes, it takes a little to get people to subscribe to your email list, but once you have them, it doesn't cost anything to attach an affiliate link to your email and send it to your subscribers. Posting in Facebook groups is another way to promote products or services for free. Join Facebook groups that are within your niche and start building relationships with the people in the group. Once you've gained their trust, you can start promoting by recommending what you want to sell using your affiliate links. If your medium is YouTube, any affiliate links that you attach to the description of the video will cost you nothing. Create your video content, talk about an issue, and present the solution. Don't forget to tell your audience where to find the link!

Share Content Everywhere

This strategy is similar to the previous one in that you should use all the free resources available to promote your content. But you should also try to get your content promoted everywhere you can when it comes to platforms. We've discussed SEO and how you can rank well in search engine results. However, you should try to go beyond SEO and use social media, email, or any other platforms, such as Medium. What you're looking for here is for your content to be exposed to the largest possible number of people.

Become Data-Driven

As you know, data is crucial in affiliate marketing, and if you want to succeed, becoming a data-driven affiliate marketer is absolutely necessary. While your data will not be available right at the start of your journey, you can always use more general data to create a plan based on the data found and go from there. As soon as you start putting out content of your own, you will get access to more accurate data related to you.

Advanced Affiliate Marketing Strategies

While basic affiliate marketing strategies can be really useful to get your career off the ground, it is with more advanced strategies that you are going to start making a difference and increasing your profit. It's fundamental that you learn the basic techniques before you start with these ones, so make sure you go through them and test them because you're still going to use them throughout your affiliate marketing career.

Owning All the Search Engine Results Page

When you've found a really profitable product or service, you should try and create various websites around that niche for you to be able to "catch" all the users interested in it. This strategy is more based on creating your content around certain products or keywords. The goal is to create several articles or pieces of content around the same item and own the entire Search Engine Results Page (SERP). This way, any piece of content the user clicks on in their results will have an affiliate link from you. The reason this works is that potential customers like to visit several pages before purchasing something, and so by creating great content and ranking higher in the SERP, you have much higher chances of making a sale. It's quite hard, if not outright impossible, to fill the whole of the first page with your affiliate links (unless the product is really niche), but you can try to have as many as you possibly can. For best results, you should try to narrow down your keywords to less competitive ones and promote evergreen content. You might also want to create websites or pieces of content for adjacent products or services so you can build up links a lot faster, as well as negotiate sponsorships with certain brands.

Set Up Proper Affiliate Tracking

While we've talked about tracking your affiliate links, there are many strategies you can use to do this; some are more complex than others, but they yield much better results. We've established that using more than one affiliate program can bring you more profits, but keeping track of all those links can be a tough task. There are two things that you can do to make this a lot easier.

The first is to aggregate sales. You can do this by using a spreadsheet and typing in the results manually. Here, you will write down the profit from each affiliate program you're using, but there are tools to make it far easier. For instance, you can use an affiliate dashboard that allows you to have an overview of the networks you're using and saves you time by eliminating the need to log everything into a spreadsheet.

Then, you can use SubID tracking. This essentially gives you more room for data from your affiliate links by adding commissions that happen as a result of a click on your affiliate link. In sum, you will have a much better perspective on what content and links are actually converting into sales. This adds a component to an affiliate link, allowing for additional data collection. For example, an affiliate link might look something like this:

756n.net/?aid=affiliate478&mid=merchant902&subid=button&url=thisisanexample.com.

This has no meaning for you, but each part of this link tells a story. For example, the "756n.net/" is usually the tracking domain; the "?aid=affiliate478" is the affiliate identifier; the "mid=merchant902" is the merchant identifier; and the "&url=thisisanexample.com" is the deep link, which leaves us with the "&subid=button" as the add SubID.

This bit of the affiliate link can give you great data to explore and make adjustments to your strategy. There are many tools that you can add to your affiliate link, but Tapfiliate is a great one.

Get On-Page Optimization

When we talk about on-page optimization, we are essentially talking about improving some of the metrics, such as the click-through rate and overall conversion. Optimizing your pages will increase your chances of making sales. But which metrics should you be concerned about?

One of the first things that you should optimize is to increase the number of affiliate links within your content. The more strategically placed affiliate links you have, the more likely your audience will click on them. However, we need to emphasize the word "well-placed," because if you're just adding affiliate links for the sake of having more, then it won't work. Your goal is to create a balance between great quality and well-placed affiliate links. Similarly, make your affiliate links visible in your content. While well-placed links are a great start, if you don't make them stand out, people will simply skim over them. Not only should your affiliate links stand out but also your CTA buttons, too. Here you can play more with graphics and colors to make them more eye-catching for the users.

Part of optimizing your pages is something that we've mentioned previously: adding an exit-intent pop-up. They are there to give one last chance to the user to click on the affiliate links before moving away from the page. You can add deals or limited offers to that pop-up. And of course, another way to optimize your page is by including social proof. This includes testimonials or customer reviews, for example. These are great ways to tell your audience that other people have enjoyed your content and purchased products or services because of your recommendation.

Be More Efficient at Promoting Your Products and Services

Once you've found a great product that is selling well, efficient promotion will increase your traffic so you can continue to sell and reach new highs. And here, you should be looking for a high volume of small to medium commissions as well as building interconnected content, such as articles that reference and link to one another.

However, this is not the only thing that will increase your sales. Certain brands convert better than others, and this is what you need to look out for. For instance, high-converting brands have a great user interface (UI), which makes it a lot easier for users to log in or sign up and purchase their services or products. Brands, where it gets too complicated to do these basic things, tend to have fewer conversions. Also, the brand's website should be optimized for mobile since almost everything now happens on users' mobiles, as well as be well designed. Another way to understand if a certain service or product converts well is to check with your competition and find out how much they promote it.

While this works best if you're promoting highly recognizable brands, sometimes that won't be the case, and you'll have to promote brands that are not as well-known. You can still promote them well and increase the conversion rate. For example, when creating content, you need to introduce the brand to your audience through it. Discuss everything you can about the brand or the product, from shipping to customer service to the refund policy and your personal experience with the brand.

Another thing that might affect your commissions is the average order value of the product or service you're promoting. Certain affiliate programs will tell you the average order value so you can estimate your commission. While this is not necessarily detrimental, it's always good to know this information so you can pick your strategies better. However, paired up with the volume of the product or service sold, you can then reach more concrete conclusions. You can always predict the volume of products by using data analytic tools to search for volume or buyer intent. To calculate it, on the other hand, you have to take your content that ranks first and the volume of traffic that is being driven. Add in the conversion rate, and you have a great estimate of the volume.

Create an Affiliate Marketing Funnel

An affiliate marketing funnel can be a great help through the many stages of the user journey until purchase by addressing many of their needs. However, you might be wondering what an affiliate marketing funnel really is. It is essentially a thorough path designed to help the user progress from a simple buyer prospect to an actual buyer in the shortest amount of time possible. When you're creating these affiliate marketing funnels, you are customizing the user's path and creating more value for them at the same time.

There are four different stages of a user's journey: Awareness is when the user sees the problem and understands it; consideration is when the user starts looking for solutions; conversion is when the user makes the decision to purchase the solution; and loyalty is when, after purchase, the customer has a great experience and it's likely they'll purchase again.

To do this, you have to use many different mediums to reach the customer and convert them. For example, in the awareness section, you want to drive traffic through social media posts, paid advertising, and SEO blog posts. The user will then proceed to the consideration phase, during which you must offer solutions, which are typically in the form of email courses, free ebooks, webinars, or anything else that provides real-value information. The following phase is conversion, also known as the warm-up phase, in which you create email sequences and bridge pages to convert the user to a buyer, and finally, the pitch, which can be done through sales emails, for example—a definitive way to make the user purchase the product or service. So, to sum up, in the first phase, you're solely driving traffic; in the second phase, you're converting that traffic through free information and solutions; and what you're looking for is to make them subscribe to your email list; then, in the third phase, you warm up the audience to then finally pitch the sale.

By creating an affiliate marketing funnel, you reach a broader audience, increasing your conversion rates, increasing your brand's trust and authority, increasing your affiliate commissions, and also increasing repeat sales.

Building a More Efficient Email List

An email list is the most straightforward way to communicate with your audience, although many affiliate marketers tend to simply send emails that do not resonate with their audience. You need to create a connection with your audience, so the emails sent need to be exactly tailored for that and not simply generic-content emails. Remember that here, you're no longer in the awareness stage, and your audience has already shown some interest. To make your emails more engaging, try to offer special sales or promotions by giving them access through a code, as long as it's authorized by the brand or the affiliate program. Some networks or brands do this quite often, so make sure you take advantage of those promotions.

If you're offering a free ebook, make sure you advertise it in your emails and ask for feedback on it. This is a great way to get to know your audience a little better. Also, if you're promoting through a blog, make sure you create exclusive content for your subscribers and not only open content for everyone. Those who subscribe should be rewarded. If ebooks are not what you're going for, you can try to give information to your audience in the form of an email course or newsletter. What you're trying to do here is get your audience to subscribe to your email list and get exclusive information.

Choose Affiliate Programs With Recurring Commissions

At this point, you've optimized your page and created an affiliate marketing funnel. So, you can move on to choosing affiliate programs that pay recurring commissions. Recurring commissions mean that the program keeps paying you as long as the customer has repeated sales and uses your link. This is as opposed to a one-off commission that every time counts as a new commission. Recurring commissions bring you many benefits because they ensure a predictable income stream every month.

It works as a compound effect as long as you continue to expand your website's traffic and those customers continue to pay for the product or service. However, you need to put more effort into retaining customers since that's the whole purpose of recurring commissions.

Email marketing is perhaps the best way to keep in touch with your audience on a regular basis while presenting them with affiliate links.

Some of the affiliate programs we've already mentioned have recurring commissions, such as ConvertKit, with a 30% recurring rate and a cookie duration of 90 days. Shopify, ActiveCampaign, and Affilimate are other great options.

Run Recurring Campaigns

Paid promotions can bring quite a lot of traffic, but as you know, exploring your free options is also a good strategy. And within this strategy, retargeting on Instagram or Facebook can be a great way to bring back customers. However, make sure that even after this, you're still making a profit because there's no point in paying $10 to reacquire a customer if they will only bring in $5 in commission.

You can do this by using the retargeting campaigns to go to a different landing page (still affiliate) that promotes the same services and products as the one where the customers first discovered you. However, be careful not to sign up for paid advertising (where you pay) through merchant sites unless it is intentional. It will be important to read the terms, conditions and fine print before signing up!

Put More Effort on Items That Are Working Now

You should focus on the items that are working for you before you decide to move on to something else or add more products to your store. If you find that your strategy so far has been sustainable, then it's probably time to scale it.

You can accomplish this in two ways: by creating content centered on the products that are performing well and by running experiments on the content that is generating the most traffic.

For the first way, you pick products that are already selling well, so what you need to do is promote them more by creating more content with more affiliate links, which increases the chances of sales. You can also create content that guides the customer through all the phases, from awareness to loyalty (if in doubt, check above for the type of content used in each stage). If you want to try the second method, you will have to run tests on the content that brings in the most traffic. Because of this, it is a lot easier to collect data and analyze it. There are many things that you can do, from placing power words around your affiliate links to changing images (if you have any in your content), highlighting the call-to-action button, changing its location, etc. These experiments don't have to be massive since the content is already bringing in great traffic, but a small refresh on the page will keep it going.

Tips to Get You Started

Many of the things that we've talked about so far in this book are great for beginners, and certainly some are great tips that you can use at the beginning of your affiliate marketing career. But before we dive into other matters about affiliate marketing, we wanted to give you some of the best tips that we didn't have the opportunity to mention until now.

Disclose Your Affiliate Links

One thing that is not often mentioned in any affiliate marketing guide is to disclose any affiliate links to your audience. As you know, you want to build trust with your audience, and one of the things that breaks trust is the use of undisclosed affiliate links. You want to tell them that you are getting paid to promote certain products or services that you talk about in your content. You don't want them to find it elsewhere because they will then doubt your integrity, which is much harder to restore afterward. In fact, if you don't disclose it, you're breaking a Federal Trade Commission (FTC) rule. There are many ways to do this. You can simply tell your audience that some of the links in your content are affiliate links, or, for instance, if you're going to use hashtags, you can use #ad. Alternatively, you can also write a disclaimer, but make sure you make it clear at the beginning of your content.

Updating Your Content Regularly

Updating your content once in a while not only saves you time but also increases the quality of your content because you improve the things that don't necessarily work and keep it updated with the latest news about the products or services. This is especially good for product or service reviews. These are constantly changing, and by updating, you're adding more information to your content.

Become an Influencer Marketer

While years ago brands had no problem working with any affiliate marketers that showed interest, nowadays they are quite selective, both through affiliate programs and direct partnerships with affiliate marketers. One of the main reasons has to do with influencers and affiliate marketing. Now companies have more to choose from than an affiliate marketer; they can go for an influencer that might give them the exposure they need. That's why combining these two professions has gone well. However, this does not mean if you're not an influencer you can't succeed as an affiliate marketer; in fact, you can do it by optimizing and expanding your audience regardless of the medium you use. You just have to focus on getting more traffic so brands will want to work with you for exposure.

If you would like to learn more about becoming a successful influencer, take a look at our book, *Social Media Influencer: The Ultimate Guide to Building a Profitable Social Media Influencer Career,* once you've mastered affiliate marketing!

Know Your Value

When brands finally offer to partner with you, make sure you know your value. This is one of the most common mistakes newcomers make. They accept a low monetary value for their services. Understanding the terms and conditions of the offer proposed is quite important. Most affiliate programs and brands only pay if a user purchases a product, although there are others that pay referral fees if the user clicks on the link or simply adds the product or service to the cart. So, by knowing exactly what you are getting paid for, you can try and negotiate your terms with the brand. Depending on your following and experience, you need to make sure you don't get underpaid by the brand, and for that, you also need to look at the prices of the products or services that you are promoting and the size of the company. However, money shouldn't always be on your mind. As an affiliate marketer, you come up with solutions for your audience and present them with high-quality information, and that's the first thing that you should be worried about. Because if you do this well, sales will certainly start coming. Remember, most affiliate programs give rewards to their most productive affiliate marketers, so you have to help as many people as possible find the solutions they need.

In the next chapter, we will focus on tools and software that will make your life a lot easier when it comes to succeeding as an affiliate marketer. There are many tools out there that change many aspects of the industry. We will divide those and explore what they do, as well as give you examples of tools and software that you can use.

Checklist

	Shop around for commission rates
	Build connections with your audience and community
	Find a mentor
	Diversify your affiliate programs and have more on hand
	Look into brand partnerships
	Add affiliate links where most of your traffic is located and disclose your affiliate links
	Customize links for different countries
	Share your content across different platforms

	Use data and analytics to plan future content and update your content regularly
	Become familiar with advanced affiliate marketing strategies and see which ones work for you
	Look into influencer marketing
	Know your value and don't be afraid to negotiate your terms

Chapter 6:

Tools and Software for the Affiliate Marketer

Affiliate marketing is an industry that has been growing substantially over the years. The more the internet and technology in general evolve, the more tools, software, and strategies are created to help affiliate marketers and brands attract more customers to purchase their products and services.

Some of the software and tools we will talk about here are essential for you to increase your return on investment, have more control over your content and affiliate links, or even generate higher-quality leads through data analysis. We will start with what we think are some of the best free tools and software for affiliate marketing. If you're just starting out, you should begin by trying out the free tools and maximizing your returns with them before you move on to paid software and tools.

Even free affiliate marketing tools have great advantages that you can explore. For instance, you have great streamlining software, tools that not only collect data but also help you manage it, and of course, also help you track links. It's also important to note that while some of these tools are completely free, others have trial periods after which you will have to pay to continue using the tool or software.

Free Affiliate Tools and Software

We've also divided the tools and software into categories to help you navigate them easily.

Tools for Content Ideas

These tools are great for giving you ideas for your content, regardless of the type of content you make.

CoSchedule's Headline Analyzer

This is a headline analyzer. As the name implies, this tool ensures you have a great headline that can rank higher on SERP. It also helps you make your headline viral and drive more traffic to your content. This tool also analyzes data to compare it and give you the best suggestions for coming up with a better headline. It focuses on word balance, sentiment, word count, headline type, clarity, and reading grade level. It's also very simple to use, and you can download it as a free plug-in for your browser.

BuzzSumo

BuzzSumo is a great tool to find trending content over different time periods. You can adjust the filter and find out what was the most popular content last year, in the last three months, or even in the last 24 hours. Besides showing you the most visited content, it also gives you other information, such as the most shared content and what type of content has been trending, among many other interesting things.

Feedly

There's no better way to get inspired to create new content than getting exposed to a large amount of it. This is exactly what Feedly is for. This tool helps you organize all the feeds from new content so you can keep track of everything, and it also shares insights from the sources you've collected. In sum, it is a great content organizer that can really increase your productivity when analyzing content.

Portent's Content Idea Generator

This tool is not very different from CoSchedule's headline analyzer, but instead of analyzing the data from headlines to create one, it simply comes up with very funny and smart headlines. You can visit their website, type in the subject you want to talk about, and then click on

"Generate Idea". It can also help you come up with content to write if you are out of ideas, since most of the time all we need is a title for an idea to come to us.

Tools for Social Media and Email Marketing

Buffer

This tool allows you to automate all of your social media updates, giving you more time to focus on the other important tasks that an affiliate marketer must complete. With this, the tool also helps you grow your audience on social media organically, as well as makes it easier to collaborate and get more clicks.

GetResponse

GetResponse is a tool that allows you to communicate better with your audience. This can be done through chats, emails, webinars, and landing pages that the tool can also build for you. You can choose from several templates that you can easily edit and make more unique and tailored to your style. Besides email marketing, it's also a website builder and a marketing automation tool.

Tools for Link Tracking and Link Creation

Bit.ly

Chances are that you've heard of this tool before because it's extremely useful. In sum, it shortens your links, which can bring a much better aesthetic to your content. Besides that, you can also generate QR codes and link-in-bios. It's extremely simple to use, and once you start, we are sure it will be one of the tools that you will use the most.

Linktrack

This tool allows you to check all the data referring to your affiliate links, such as revenue, number of clicks, etc. With an extremely well-designed dashboard, you can get all the data in one place. It also has a paid version where you get more advanced options and other data that you can check. However, if what you want is the most basic information, you can go for the free version of the tool.

Google's URL Builder

This tool is part of Google Analytics software, but it's designed specifically to track social media posts and advertisements. It's quite easy to use; you can enter the URL from the website and campaign information, such as the campaign ID, source, medium, or name. Then, you will be presented with a table with everything there is to know about the campaign and ads.

Tools for SEO

This will probably be the largest list since SEO is such an important subject in the affiliate world. There are many different tools and software programs that you can use and combine to rank your pages higher. Let's have a look at some of those tools.

Google Search Console

This is another Google tool and one of the very first keyword software to ever exist. It gives you basic information about keywords such as traffic, issues, performance, etc. As with most Google tools, you will need a Google Ads account, but because of all the other tools that you can use with that account, you should have one anyway. The Google Search Console might not have the most advanced filters and technology when compared to newer tools, even from Google, but it's certainly an easy-to-use software that is extremely reliable. We recommend you use it and get familiar with it because it will come in handy.

Mangools Google SERP Simulator

This is a preview tool that allows you to check how an article would appear on the SERP. This is important because we want to see what the users see when they perform a search on Google. Is the title engaging and appealing enough to look at? Is the little prompt good enough? With this tool, you can preview it before you publish it. This is also a free tool. Simply go to the website and enter the URL, title, description, and bold keywords. You also have the option to preview it on a desktop or mobile device. It's quite a great little tool that can make your life much easier.

Google Search Central

You might have heard of this tool under a different name called Google Webmasters. If not, this is a great tool that helps you find the right audience to show your content to and makes your content and your websites easier to find for the right people. However, with Google Search Central, you can do so much more. You need to create an account, then connect all your websites and content to it. That way, you will be able to use every single tool Google Search Central has, such as data analytics and PageSpeed Insights, to check the speed of your websites, optimize your pages in the SERP, or even check how mobile-friendly your pages are. There's plenty more you can do with this tool, and even if it takes a little getting used to, it's certainly worth it.

Majestic SEO

This is another data-analysis SEO tool, but one that has been used by many affiliate marketers in the past. Although it doesn't bring anything new to the table when compared to other SEO and keyword data tools, it's extremely reliable and easy to use. You can simply type in the keyword or URL and get all sorts of data from your or your competitors' websites.

Fruition's Google Penalty Checker

One of the most perplexing aspects of Google searches is the Google Algorithm Updates. Sometimes you work hard to get ranked high on SERPs, and then Google updates its algorithm, and you're no longer in the top results of Google searches. Although this tool will not stop any of that, it will tell you exactly what happened in the update and why you've dropped in rank, so you can make changes and climb back up.

Free Assets

Sometimes you just need a great picture to fill in the blanks on your latest article blog. There are a few websites where you can simply search and download pictures at no extra cost because those images are copyright free. That essentially means that you can use them without paying or even without the authorization of the photographer or designer.

Because all of the free websites do the same thing, we will simply list them:

- Death to the Stock Photo
- Unsplash
- Giphy
- Pixabay
- Pexels

Free Tools for Ads and Optimization

Now these tools will really come in handy, as they offer many different solutions for problems that you will certainly face. Campaigns are something that we will explore in the next chapter, so after you read them, make sure you come back to this section to learn how to use them once you launch your own campaign.

Ad Comparator

Campaigns require quite some work on your behalf, even for the most seasoned affiliate marketers out there. There are just too many things that you need to do, and you often do them all by yourself. Well, Ad Comparator cannot help you with all the different things that you have to deal with, but it can help you with the budget for ads as well as help you test different approaches. With this tool, you can save some money, increase conversion rates, and optimize your marketing activities.

TubeBuddy

If your chosen type of content is videos, in particular videos on your YouTube channel, then TubeBuddy is a great tool to optimize your videos. It will optimize your keywords and titles to allow you to reach a broader audience, as well as rank you in terms of SEO, so you can see exactly where you're at and improve from there.

Free Tools for Content Editors

Canva

This is quite a popular content editor that allows you to edit images, videos, and webpages, and it has many other tools to design proper content. While it has a free trial, it's not completely free, but it's quite affordable.

It also has a massive template library of everything they offer, as well as a tight community. It's definitely worth trying it out, and if you like it, you can even purchase it.

VN Video Editor

This is another video editor, but unlike other editors where it takes some time for you to get used to it, with VN, there's hardly a steep curve when it comes to getting you started. While it's fairly easy to use, it still gives you plenty of great tools and professional features to bring your videos to life. Another advantage of this video editor is that it comes in two versions: mobile and desktop.

Paid Affiliate Tools and Software

Now, once you've taken advantage of all the free tools and free trials of the tools we've listed just above but still feel like you might need something more to be able to compete in the industry, you might be looking for paid software or tools. Something that can really improve your output and drive sales.

MobileMonkey

MobileMonkey is a chatbot, and you might be wondering why you would want a chatbot on your website. Well, they can grow every aspect of your affiliate marketing. This is live chat software that is able to coherently engage with your audience, generate more leads, and increase your profit.

However, chatbots are mostly seen on a company's (in this case, a merchant's) website, although depending on the type of website you have, they can be a great addition to increasing engagement rates.

Voluum

Voluum is an ad-tracking software that is specifically designed to help affiliate marketers track their advertisements. Not only that, but you also have access to a huge amount of data and other insights, as well as the ability to optimize the performance of your advertising.

Voluum allows you to use the software on most platforms, and it offers a large number of templates that you can choose from, besides supporting a long list of advertising types such as video, social media, email, search, display, pop-up, and more.

AffJet

If you work with numerous affiliate programs (as you should), AffJet can analyze the different performances of each network and place them all in one place. Not only that, but the software also allows you to increase commissions. To get started, you can add the affiliate programs you use and transfer all the data you have from those programs into AffJet.

There, the application provides one of the most sophisticated filters, allowing you to go through your data and properly analyze it. It also has the ability, after you've filtered all the data properly, to create detailed reports for ease of comprehension.

AdPlexity

AdPlexity is one of the best tools for ad intelligence. If you are unfamiliar with the terms, ad intelligence tracks the advertising activities of several brands, such as your competitors, as well as other companies in the industry. Essentially, with this software, you can know everything that has to do with how much money brands are spending on advertising and where they are spending this money.

This particular software is extremely versatile and tracks ads on several devices, such as mobile, desktop, ecommerce, etc. For example, if we look at the mobile section of AdPlexity, you can check the most profitable advertising campaigns of your competitors, their traffic sources, clicks, and more, so you can make much better decisions with your campaigns.

With AdPlexity, you can access campaigns in over 75 countries, download competitor landing pages, and get real-time information about campaigns running on all devices. You can also find campaigns by simply searching by keyword, publisher, advertiser, or affiliate program, so it's quite easy to get used to.

Zeropark

Zeropark is another excellent tool for ad campaigns, as long as you enjoy managing your own. Essentially, the app allows you to manage and launch campaigns in many different formats, such as in-page push, pop-up, in-app, and more. One of the best advantages of this app is that you can find out if some of the new products or services that you're adding are good enough to invest more money in and if they have conversion power.

However, probably the best thing about Zeropark is how fast their campaign approval is. As you might know, campaigns on large social media platforms such as Instagram or Facebook can take some time to be approved, which won't happen if you use this tool. Although keep in mind that it can still be denied.

Flippa

Affiliate marketers must always be on the lookout for new opportunities and be able to build new websites from the ground up if they decide to launch a new product or service or if they want to specialize in a different niche and build a website to create new content. Whatever it is that you are looking for, one of the main issues is looking for domains, and this is exactly what Flippa does: it finds domains in the marketplace, where you can simply find domains that already exist and are up for sale. The tool also shows you a large array of data, such as the domain authority score.

It's a great tool if you want to buy an already-made domain with some online presence, so you don't have to start from scratch.

Unbounce

This is a great tool to build landing pages quickly and efficiently. Even if you don't know anything about coding, you can use Unbounce because of how simple it is. Besides that, it has a few features, such as Smart Traffic or Conversion Intelligence, that are excellent for increasing your traffic and conversions.

Landing pages are essential when you're running campaigns that target specific niches. So, when your campaigns are active, you need to be able to build great landing pages for whatever products or services you're promoting. Also, landing pages are an important part of marketing funnels, as we've seen. You can even A/B test different landing pages to understand which ones work best with your campaign.

Rebrandly

Rebrandly is a link-tracking tool, although if we compare it to the free tools for link tracking we've mentioned before, none comes close to this. While most link-tracking tools track links, Rebrandly does that but also offers link cloaking, which allows you to essentially hide your affiliate URL from others as well as shorten your affiliate link. By shortening the affiliate link, you are also making it more appealing to users, as well as more noticeable.

It also offers more comprehensive analytical tools compared to its free counterparts, as well as more customization, including adding your brand name to your links. They also offer a Google Chrome extension, so it's extremely versatile and easy to use.

ThirstyAffiliates

This is another link-cloaking tool that can work in combination with Rebrandly because it's a simple WordPress plug-in. If you often use WordPress, this tool is what you need if you want to focus on link cloaking. It doesn't have as many features, but it's worth it.

Thrive Leads

If you're having trouble building up your mailing list, then Thrive Leads is a great tool that can help you. It's also a WordPress plug-in and lead generation software. A drag-and-drop system makes it extremely simple to create good designs. Besides that, it also has other features, such as increasing conversions by showing your audience sales and offers.

Affiliate Tools for Specific Platforms

Social media is a large part of what makes affiliate marketing successful, so it's only normal that some affiliate marketing tools are specifically designed to work on certain social media platforms. There are other important platforms, such as Amazon, that contribute a lot to the affiliate marketing area. Let's have a look at some of them.

Tailwind

Tailwind is considered a social media marketing tool that allows you to schedule, as well as analyze, any data from Instagram and Pinterest. Picture-based content is extremely important for generating leads and sales of physical products, so if this is your niche, Tailwind could be the tool for you.

Among many other features, Tailwind offers a hashtag finder, content plans, visual planning, free landing pages, and clickable links. It also offers clean reports of all the data you are able to collect.

Amazon Affiliate WordPress Plug-in

You might already know what platform this plug-in is used for—yes, Amazon. The Amazon Affiliate WordPress Plug-in, often simply written as AAWP, is a tool that constantly updates the information on Amazon. As you might know, Amazon has too many products to keep track of, so with this tool, you have updated information with extremely easy access. As a result, whenever a product's price is reduced or increased, the tool updates; the same is true for offers or other discounts. AAWP offers more features, such as marketing automation, but up-to-date information is certainly the reason this tool is so popular among affiliate marketers.

MobileMonkey for SMS

While it's not as popular nowadays, some affiliate marketers still like to promote their products and services through SMS. MobileMonkey, which we've already mentioned in this chapter, also has this feature. It works like email marketing, where you can send SMS in bulk to all your user lists, but you can also automate SMS drip campaigns as well as automated responses to other messages.

Pods by Quuu

While Quuu is a company that produces great tools for marketing on social media platforms, one of their latest tools—Pods—is what we will talk about here. Pods allow the automation of shared content through different social media platforms. Essentially, you can share content among your contacts and friends seamlessly.

Once you sign up for Quuu, you can connect any social media scheduling plug-in or software you use, then create a "pod," and the tool will handle everything for you. Even better, this tool allows for the organic sharing of content, so you won't have any problem with social media platforms taking it down.

MeetEdgar

Evergreen content is something that you create that is always relevant, even if a long time has passed. And this marketing tool is what is called a "recycler," which automates the sharing of this type of content across many different social media platforms such as Instagram, Twitter, Facebook, etc.

It also works as a content scheduler, but you only need to upload the content you want once, and it will share it automatically. As this repeatedly shares the content, it increases the chances of more users seeing it and expanding your audience.

Agorapulse

Social media management can get a lot easier if you use Agorapulse. This tool consolidates all of your social media pages into a single dashboard for easy management. It gives you all the metrics from all your social media platforms in easy-to-read reports, so you can make better decisions.

In fact, analyzing data and reports is one of the strongest features of Agorapulse, with various metrics that you can simply download.

Analisa.io

TikTok has become one of the largest social media platforms in the world, and it's obvious that someone was going to create software to specifically target and analyze its content. Analisa is that tool, and it's quite easy to use. It's AI-powered and analyzes TikTok profiles through followers, hashtags, and profiles. But it also has many more tools that you can use to get more accurate readings, such as influencer mapping, historical data, content engagement, tagged relationships, and more.

PhantomBuster

PhantomBuster is a tool dedicated to automation and data extraction for social media platforms. This tool offers more than 200 automated actions on the most diverse social media platforms, from LinkedIn to

Facebook or even Quora. All of these automations can be individualized, meaning that if you're working with different platforms, you can use a certain automation on one social media platform and a different one on another and properly create and design your strategies.

Brand24

This is a tool that allows you to increase your brand's reputation across different social media platforms. Not only that, but you can also track your competitors' reputations, monitor your own, and manage them online. It can also check for any mentions of your brand on different channels across the web.

So if you're looking to improve your brand, measure your PR efforts, get automated reports, or improve customer satisfaction, Brand24 is a great tool to use.

AddThis

AddThis uses an easy-to-use drag-and-drop system that allows you to share all your content in no time. You can use this tool on any social media platform, and while sharing is its main purpose, AddThis also comes with other tools for increasing traffic, connecting email inboxes, and building up your user base through follow buttons. It's quite handy if you're looking for more engagement.

This is a list of some of the best tools you can find for affiliate marketing. As we've said, you should take advantage of all the free tools and trials you can before choosing paid tools and software. Get familiar with those and try to maximize your productivity with them. Paid tools are designed to bring you even more sales and profit, but you need to have a solid foundation and knowledge before paying for them, or it would simply be a waste of money.

In the following chapter, we will talk about how you can launch and optimize your campaign and where some of these tools will come in handy. We will talk about it from a step-by-step perspective to make it easier to follow.

Checklist

	Do research on different free and paid affiliate tools and software
	Decide on the best tools and software for your medium and platforms

Chapter 7:

Launching Your Campaign

If you've been reading, you know quite a bit about affiliate marketing. It's now time to learn how you can launch your own campaign. This is simply a more elaborate way to generate more sales and profit from promoting products or services. It entails everything we've already discussed but done in a specific order to help you reach your goal faster and more effectively.

Keep in mind that while we can talk about campaigns from an affiliate marketer's point of view, most marketing campaigns are launched by brands. Now, you can adopt the role of a brand and continue working as an affiliate marketer, but one that wants to build its brand and that has its own products. In this case, you will be taking on the role of a merchant, even if it's to grow your affiliate marketer audience. With this, you might have to work with affiliate programs and networks and even find more affiliate marketers to promote your products or services.

Steps to Launch Your Affiliate Marketing Campaign

There are quite a few steps that you need to follow, but we will list them in order so you can fully understand the process.

Pick a Traffic Source

While you don't want all your eggs in one basket, you also don't want to have your traffic spread thinly over a too wide range of sources. Instead, you might want to pick a few traffic sources and really focus on them. We suggest three to four different traffic sources since it's better to be good at a few of them than bad at all of them.

Some of the more popular traffic sources include email marketing, SEO strategy, social media advertising, PPC advertising, and contextual advertising. Your picks should be related to the type of product or service you promote, the type of content used, and your audience.

Choose Offer Categories

Offer categories are simply offers of products or services that you promote, which are also called "verticals." As you know, there are a myriad of niches to choose from, and you need to do your research to understand the level of competition, the size of the audience, and the commissions. For that, you need to find out what your audience actually wants. The best way to find that out is to use some of the tools we've mentioned before, such as Facebook Audience Insights, BuzzSumo, etc.

You will also have to apply for affiliate programs that match the niche you've chosen. Try to apply for as many programs as you can because these companies usually take some time before replying, and their answer can also be a negative one. After you're in a program, you will be able to check out quite a few offers. The number of offers you receive will be determined by the program you choose and the niche you are in. Make sure you choose wisely and that what you are going to promote is exactly what you want to do and aligns with your type of affiliate marketing.

Even after you've been accepted into an affiliate program, there are some requirements that you need to fulfill during the time you're there. For instance, you will have to send valid traffic that aligns with the rules of the program. If you don't do that, the chances of getting banned from the program increase. Some requirements include the type of traffic, such as banners and pop-ups; the country that traffic comes from - some programs only accept traffic from certain countries; and whether or not the program accepts traffic from adult websites, such as bespoke liquor blogs or online gambling sites.

Purchasing matching traffic is the next thing you should do after you've chosen the traffic sources. When you purchase traffic, what you're actually doing is bidding to try and get a specific segment of the traffic that matches exactly what you need. With this, you can advertise to your matching audience and not to a random audience that has no interest in the products or services you are promoting. The size of the audience you're targeting should also be taken into consideration because you can simply bid more money to get a larger audience, although that might decrease the effectiveness of the campaign and, with it, your profitability since you're paying more money to reach a larger audience and probably selling less. Essentially, you have to think about the quality of your audience.

Designing Landing Pages

A crucial part of launching a campaign is building great landing pages. Once a user in your audience clicks on the affiliate link, they will be led to a landing page that has to be excellent, or you might lose that customer and a sale. While the design is important, what's more important is to display the right information to potential customers. You don't want prospective customers to land on a page that has little to do with what they are looking for; instead, you want to make sure the link leads exactly to what you've advertised.

Setting up Backend

This essentially means that you will need to set up your tracking links properly. You also have to keep an eye on it at all times because if you only rely on the information given to you by affiliate programs, you are going to have many holes in the full data available, which might impair your decisions. By setting up trackers, you will be able to understand how you're making money and not just how much you're making. For instance, you will have better knowledge of what segments of your audience have a better response to your campaign, what are the best landing pages, and even what hours of the day are more profitable to you.

While you can do this manually with a spreadsheet, it's a lot of work and takes a lot of time. However, tracking is much faster and easier to set up, and it gives you all the information you need. As you might remember, we gave examples of many different types of tools that track. Voluum is perhaps the most complete tool in the list, but you also have free ones that can give you some important information too.

Launching Your Campaign

You've picked your traffic source, chosen your vertical, designed the landing pages necessary, and set up your tracking and links; now it's time to launch your campaign. Launching an affiliate marketing campaign is similar to launching a service, product, or piece of software; if you do it wrong, all your efforts will be compromised. You need to understand when the best time is to launch your campaign, and that's why you've acquired so much data. You need to know the best day and the best hour to launch your campaign on the most diverse platforms. If these are poorly timed, your whole campaign might not have the desired effect. If you assume that the majority of people use social media platforms during the day and late evening (depending on the day of the week, of course), you have quite a big window to launch your campaign. It's also a good idea to combine your launch with large events (if it makes sense with the products or services you're promoting).

Optimizing Your Affiliate Marketing Campaign

Now that you know how to launch an affiliate marketing campaign, you will need to know how to optimize it, just as you have to do in your solo affiliate marketing efforts. When doing this, there are two main things that you need to focus on: the conversion rate and the quality of traffic.

Optimizing for Quality of Traffic

As with everything surrounding affiliate marketing, you need to analyze your customer and revenue data to fully understand the quality of traffic you're getting. Ask yourself these questions: What is the value of a new customer? What about a repeat customer? What is the definition of lifetime value? Or what are the different profit margins for the different products you have? All of this data can be collected through the many tools we've mentioned.

From a merchant point of view, if you're connecting with other affiliates to expand your audience and promote your own products (even if these are more promotional contents, such as a blog or YouTube channel), there are a few things that you need to know. First, as an affiliate marketer, you need to know how to choose the right affiliates for you.

You know the importance of having great affiliate marketers on your team, but finding the right ones can be quite time-consuming. However, it's a necessary thing that you will need to do if you want a successful affiliate marketing campaign. When searching for good affiliate marketers, it's important that you ask a few questions. For instance, has the affiliate marketer worked in the industry and in the niche before? What type of experience do they have, and what are they currently promoting? What websites do they have and run? What are their most popular strategies? Answering this can give you great insights into how experienced the affiliate marketers are.

After you've chosen a few, you need to have them on board. However, this is a common question on everyone's mind when they start recruiting affiliate marketers. The first thing is to get your affiliate marketers familiar with what you want to promote and what your company's values are. If you have a small affiliate program with only a few affiliate marketers, you will want to be their contact point with the program. If you are expanding and have several affiliate marketers, you need to start hiring affiliate managers, but that might take a while. What you want to do at this stage is be there for them if they need any help. Don't forget to talk to them about your brand and the voice and tone you want to project with your campaign. Then, it will be important to show them data related to your brand, such as demographics, traffic sources, and channels. The more your affiliates know about your brand, product, or service, the better they are able to perform.

Communication with your affiliates is also an important part of driving quality traffic to your websites. In fact, communication is also crucial for the happiness of an affiliate marketer in the program. If they feel like there's no communication between them and you or the affiliate manager, they often choose to leave the program. They need to feel supported and aware of what is happening. This has advantages for both you and them since they will know of any changes in your products and promote them better. If your affiliate marketers are doing well, reward them. We've talked about this in previous chapters from an affiliate marketer's perspective, but it's important to highlight it from a brand's point of view. If your affiliate marketers are performing well and closing sales, you must reward them in order for them to continue promoting your products or services and to keep them. This is also the reason tracking is important: so you know which affiliate marketers are performing well and which aren't. This will help you to properly reward them or inform you to bring in new ones.

As you know, there are a few affiliate marketing methods that affiliate marketers can use to drive traffic to their websites, although some of these might not be appropriate for your strategy or even the products you're trying to sell. You might have to restrict some methods if you think that they won't fit in with your strategy. There could be many reasons for restricting a specific type of affiliate marketing method, but the most common is that you already use that method and don't want your affiliates to use it because it could be counterproductive since you're targeting the same audience segment. You may want to restrict these methods and communicate with your affiliates to let them know of the available methods they can use.

Even if you vet your own affiliate marketers, you need to always be on the lookout for unethical behaviour from them. This could severely limit your ability to drive traffic to your websites and make sales. It is important to monitor your affiliate's activities. The most common instance of unethical behaviour is to alter or bring in inorganic traffic or use URLs that have trademark terms. This might make it seem like they are driving more traffic than they really are, which might prompt you to pay them more for their efforts. So, while they might be damaging your brand, they might also be getting paid for work that is not done.

Testing your landing pages as frequently as you can, will help to optimize your traffic too. Ideally, you would have your affiliates drive traffic to your landing pages, which makes it very easy to implement A/B tests. You'll be able to understand your conversion rates based on the traffic you're receiving this way.

Optimizing for Conversions

Now you know how to optimize to drive traffic to your landing pages, but the job is not done if you can't convert that traffic into sales. Now, what do you need to do to optimize your conversions and increase your profit?

Well, for one, you can create SMART goals. SMART stands for specific, measurable, achievable, realistic, and time-bound goals. If you're still confused, we will explain it a little better. Let's go through what these actually mean in a "goal" context.

Having well-defined and clear goals is what it means to be specific. You have to be certain of what you're after and what needs to be done. So, if you define a goal as "growing your business," that's not nearly specific enough. You could, instead, say, "I want to increase conversion" or "I want to drive more traffic to my landing pages."

Goals have to be measurable, so that you are able to quantify them in numbers. They need to be concrete, like "increase your conversion by 15%" or "increase traffic by 20%." You need to have a specific goal, not just the intention of a goal.

Achievable and realistic means considering the resources you have and understanding what goals can be considered within your limits. If you know, with the resources you have, that an increase of 30% in conversion in one month is almost impossible, that's not an achievable or realistic goal. You have to set objectives that you know you can commit to, so you don't lose focus and become demotivated. If you've set goals that are unachievable, you need to go back and reset them.

Lastly, time-bound goals have a certain time to be achieved, and this parameter is intrinsically connected with achievable and realistic parameters. You have to properly plan to understand how long it will take to reach the objective you want, but you also have to work with the resources you have to reach it. Setting SMART goals will give you direction and something to look for at the start of your campaign. You have to properly plan beforehand to make sure you don't deviate from them, so take your time when you're setting these goals for yourself.

Another thing that you can do to optimize your conversions when launching a campaign is to conduct and review customer analysis. This is something you must do throughout your campaign in order to adjust your strategies. You already have your goals set, so understanding your audience is far easier. You will know their main browsing behaviors and how willing they are to pay for products or services, etc. The more you understand your audience, the better you can optimize your campaign.

Even when looking to optimize your conversions, you have to use the same methods that you used when optimizing your traffic sources. Things like shortlisting your best affiliate marketing programs (if you're using one) and basing your optimization on the traffic sources. This is important because if you find out that a certain traffic source is not converting into sales, you might as well stop it and save the money spent on advertising and promoting through that traffic source. Another thing that you also use when optimizing traffic sources and that is extremely useful when optimizing conversions is A/B testing. You test so you can increase your ROI. Given the data you've collected, you might have to create a better CTA, change your landing pages to become more appealing, increase the loading time on your pages, etc. To summarize, in order to optimize a campaign, you must test it and be able to adapt to changes as they occur.

Other Tips to Optimize Your Campaign

There are other things that don't fall into the "optimize for quality traffic or conversions" category that can be very useful to generally optimize your campaign.

You can create or update a "tools" page that can aid your audience and let them know what tools you actually use, regardless of the niche you're in. People appreciate great tips, and even if none of the tools you list are affiliate links, it builds trust between you and your audience. However, make sure that you only list tools or other services that you use and that actually improve what you do. If some of the tools listed happen to be linked with an affiliate link, that's just a plus. Your main goal should be to present them with solutions.

Most affiliate programs have marketing resources that are usually linked to the merchant's web pages or related to them. This can be templates, logos, user guidelines, banners, and more. Make sure you take advantage of them to make your own content better and increase your sales and clicks. If you can't find that on the affiliate program's page, try reaching out to the affiliate manager, as they might be able to help you.

There's a content medium that we've not mentioned yet but that's on the rise, and that's podcasts. While it is a relatively new medium, it is quickly becoming one of the best for conversions. If podcasts are something that interests you and you think you will be good at, you should definitely give them a go. However, different podcast platforms work in various ways, so adding links can differ widely between platforms, and some are more effective than others. Just do your research to find which one is best for you and your affiliate marketing type, but a good starting point might be visiting the WordPress podcast page.

Leveraging all the built-in tools social media platforms have can lead to great things. There's a large array of tools that different social media platforms offer that not every affiliate marketer uses. You can optimize the size of the pictures you use, for example, or increase the number of shares a certain post has without using third-party tools.

Reposting your content on social media platforms that you might not use as much, such as LinkedIn or Medium, can also expand your audience and optimize your results. For instance, if blogging is your main medium for content, then Medium is an excellent choice to repost. However, in both of these platforms, there are some things you should avoid using in comparison to others, such as CTAs, because they may be considered spam. Also, avoid direct linking (even though it is permitted), because both Medium and LinkedIn attract a specific type of audience that is not used to being bombarded with advertisements as seen on Instagram or Facebook.

These tips work regardless of the niche or industry you're in, but you need to know how to choose the ones that can make the most impact with the resources you have at hand. And once again, data analysis is your best tool. You have to research and adapt your strategy as often as you can to be able to optimize every effort you make.

In the following and last chapter of this book, we will go through different methods for you to advertise your campaign. While a well-designed campaign can be a great asset, it will have no effect if it's not advertised properly. We will talk about how you can design your ads, how to use copywriting to improve your campaign, and how to thoroughly design landing pages.

Checklist

	Pick your traffic sources
	Finalize your offer categories
	Design a great landing page
	Learn how to set up tracking links in the backend of your site or profile
	Launch your campaign
	Optimize your marketing campaign

Chapter 8:

Advertising Your Campaign

In this last chapter, we will continue to talk about the main topic of the previous one: campaigns. But this time, we will explore how you can advertise your campaigns. The advertising industry is worth many billions of dollars, and affiliate marketing is but a sliver of that. However, digital advertising is the fastest-growing share of advertising, and affiliate marketing falls into the category.

That is one of the reasons why knowing how to properly advertise your campaign can yield enormous results. This is true whether you just want to advertise your affiliate links or promote your own products or services. Now, the question is, "What is the right platform or medium to advertise on?" Let's find out.

How to Create an Ad?

There are a series of steps that you need to go through to create an ad and advertise your campaign. Some of them might bear resemblance to the process you use when setting up your affiliate marketing business, but they are essential steps that you need to go through nonetheless.

Choose Your Target Audience

You should know by now who your target audience is if you've gone through it during your affiliate marketing process. However, it's recommended that you have another look, optimize, and make it clear which segment of your audience you want to target. Even within your entire audience, there might be different types of users, so make sure you create an ad that appeals to the majority of them. Go back to your buyer persona to properly define who you want to target, along with checking your data resources.

Reviewing the main points of your marketing research will also help you. Go back and reassess the main questions you have to ask, such as the age of your target audience, what are their hobbies, what platforms do they use more often, and where do they live? This is crucial later on when you're trying to figure out what type of ad and platform to use.

Choosing the Platform for Your Ads

With the data that you've acquired through market research, you should be able to pinpoint some of the best platforms to run your ads. If you still end up with too many choices, make sure you also research other things, such as ROI or ad costs, as well as the advantages and disadvantages of certain platforms.

While choosing a single platform to run your ads might be the best option, this is not always true. Sometimes it's best to use more than one since they might complement each other. Of course, that should be based on the type of campaign you're running and the platforms, what you are advertising, and your target audience. For instance, sometimes using only social media ads is the best option for you; other times, using a combination of search engine ads and banners on large retail platforms might be best. Look for where your audience is.

Decide on Your Budget

It's true that if you want to properly advertise and make money, you need to spend some too. And this is where most people fail because they tend to overlook how much it actually costs to run a successful campaign, or they are too afraid the results won't bring any real profits. Well, if done correctly, it will undoubtedly bring you profits.

There are three things that you need to plan out to clearly understand how you can budget your campaign's advertising. One is to find out the overall budget you will actually need to reach your objectives. Then, you will have to break down the costs of your spending and place them in categories. And lastly, you will have to project your ROI.

To calculate the ROI, you need to have a projection of your net income, divide it by the planned cost of investment, and multiply the result by 100. So it looks something like this:

ROI = Net Income / Cost of Investment × 100

Create Your Message

Now that you know who your target audience is, what budget you will use, and what platforms you will use to advertise your campaign, you're still missing one important part: your message.

What is it that you want your audience to do? Do you want to drive traffic to your website? Do you want them to purchase your product or service? Answering this is a good starting point to begin crafting your message. Keep in mind that a marketing message is you (or your company) talking to your audience, or what you can do to help your audience with a certain problem.

One thing to remember when creating your message is to get right to the point. Be clear and concise since people don't have time to read an entire page, and you can only capture their attention with a sentence or a small paragraph. Make sure you hit the pain points and address your audience in a clear manner. Ideally, you would also want to add a CTA at the end, but this is not mandatory.

Understanding and being empathetic with your audience can significantly generate more leads and, ultimately, sales. One of the things that your audience will seek out often is great customer service and how well the merchant "gets them." And so, looking at the problem they want to be solved through their lenses is a great way to do that.

This might take some brainstorming, but visit your website and look at the product or service you're trying to sell. Find out what message you're sending (or trying to send) to them and compare that with the problem you're trying to solve. The more you understand them, the easier it is to make sales.

The tone of your message is also important. Ideally, you want to try to be friendly and informal (however, this last one might depend on what you're trying to sell). Your message should be written in a conversational tone (you can even use slang if it's appropriate) or add a little humor to it. Being friendly will increase the trust your audience has in you and make them more likely to convert. Remember that they are human beings, so treat them as such.

As we've stated, when writing your message, be clear and concise. This often means that after they've read your sentence or small paragraph, they won't need more context or explanation to understand what your message conveys. If they are still confused or don't quite get what you mean, then that's not a well-written message. However, while getting to the point is fundamental, there are times when your message might be a little too short and lacking in coherence. Of course, the target audience you're speaking to might also contribute to the understanding of the message. You should run some tests before choosing a message and publishing it because it might not be as obvious as you think it is. For instance, if they are not aware of your brand or what your brand does, a short message might fall short in terms of meaning.

Regardless of the length of the message or the type of audience you're sending that message to, remember to be original. Being unique in the way you convey your message and in the way you write it will make your message pop out. Marketing is a very competitive industry, and while there are many original ideas out there, you will need your own original one. It's important that you are able to convey your message perfectly to your audience. Sometimes it is not even about your product or service because chances are what you're trying to sell is not that unique, and there are other people selling the same solution, but if your message speaks to your audience more than your competition, you will sell more.

One last thing that is in the same line as the last paragraph is to make the customers smile. While everyone is running around nowadays, people always have time for things that make them feel good, and that's exactly why it's important to create something that adds value to your audience. If you are able to create a positive emotion in them, they will be more likely to purchase from you.

Get People Talking

Ultimately, you want people to talk about your message and advertising. That is the reason a well-crafted message is so important. The more people talk, the more exposure it gets. This is because people will remember your brand once they need the solution you're offering. However, getting people to talk about something like an ad in today's world is not an easy task since, with the rise of social media and the internet, we are constantly bombarded with advertising and news, which makes us forget about most of the things we see. If your message can get people to stop for a second and share it with their friends and family (or even repost it), you've accomplished what you set out to do. Plus, you will also increase your chances of having more organic traffic coming to your website.

Decide What You Are Doing First

Advertising promotes two things: products or brand awareness. You need to decide which of the two you're doing first. Ideally, you might start with brand awareness and solely focus on that, then move on to product awareness. However, as an affiliate marketer, who is simply promoting other brands' products and services, you might use your campaign to promote only products.

Now, whatever you decide on pursuing, you should approach them in different ways. If you're promoting brand awareness, you want to tell the story of your brand and get your audience to know your brand and what your values are. On the other hand, if you want to promote product awareness, then you have to focus on the product itself and highlight its characteristics.

Create Test Ads

Regardless of the type of campaign, product, or brand you want to promote, you always need to first run some test ads to understand what works and what doesn't. Sometimes the design of your app simply doesn't work as well as you imagined it, or your message doesn't come across coherently. Adobe Photoshop is perhaps the best software for you to try out your ads.

It's quite simple to create ads in Photoshop, and we will show you the very basic methods. Keep in mind that this software has many other tools that can deepen your creativity and really make your ads look great, but learning everything about them takes a little bit of time. However, if you do have that time, we recommend you explore the software.

But if all you want to do is create a mock-up, you can simply open the software, select "File," and click on "New." Then, the software will prompt you to choose the size of your advertisement. You can then simply drag and drop the image you want to use into Photoshop, and if you want to add some text, you can click on the "T" on the sidebar (it's located at the end of it on your left-hand side). Then, the software will give you more options, such as color, size, and whether you want your text to be displayed vertically or horizontally. Remember to add a CTA if you think it's necessary. Again, click on the "T" on the sidebar and go through the same process.

Here's a little tip that works on most social media platforms such as Facebook, Instagram, etc. Your image should only have about 20% of the text contained in it. It will not only rank higher on the platforms, but your audience will be more drawn to it if it contains more images and less text. Then save the image. Photoshop will by default save images in .psd format, but for most social media platforms, the correct format is .png, which you can choose once you open the saving menu.

Creating Assets

When we mention assets in the advertising industry, and in this context in particular, we mean creative assets such as banner ads, landing pages, or anything else that has some advertising potential. Essentially, anything that is an ad in any way. If they have a long-form copy, such as video scripts, short-form for online ads, custom images, GIFs, photographs, or videos, they are creative assets.

Now, as part of your advertising campaign, you need to develop them. You might think that to create some of these, you need to have some sort of background, whether as a writer, designer, photographer, etc. While basic experience is necessary to create them, you can also hire people to do it for you. Ideally, you would have a team of freelancers that you can rely on to help you create these. What is important here is that you develop them so you can use them to advertise your campaign.

Determine How to Measure Your Progress

You've set your goals; now it's time to measure them, much like when you measure your own progress with affiliate marketing. And just like that, you need to answer a few things: How are you going to measure your success? And what do you call success?

We've already talked about the overall goal of your advertising campaign, but you need to track several metrics to know that you're going in the right direction. Most social media platforms have their own built-in tracking, so that's an easy thing to do. But you might also want to use some of the third-party tools we've mentioned before to better track your results. Then, select exactly what you want to track to know if you're doing it right, whether it is purchases, traffic, page likes, or how many promotional codes have been used.

Launching Your Ad

You've now gone through all the steps of advertising your campaign, and all that's left is to actually launch it. Now, different platforms have different ways to do this. For instance, the way you launch an ad on Facebook is different from launching an ad on Twitter or YouTube. That's why we are writing a step-by-step guide on how to launch your ad on all major social media platforms.

Launch Your Ad on Facebook

When you're launching an ad on Facebook, there are a myriad of things that you need to do, or better yet, boxes to tick, and this can be a little overwhelming, especially if you're doing it for the first time. We will assist you in this so that you can successfully launch your ad on the platform.

Facebook is one of the largest social media platforms in the world, and because of that, your ads can reach many people across the world and expand your audience. But the platform makes it easier for you to choose who you want to target your ads at. By setting your filters on the platform by age, hobbies, interests, or even behavior, you can easily reach the audience you seek.

The Facebook Ads Manager is the tool to launch your ad. It's quite easy to work with, and its dashboard is rather simple but has many options. Once you're in the software, there are four main categories: Summary, All Ads, Audiences, and Automated Ads.

In the Summary tab, you have some information, such as your ad performance, how much you've spent so far, and other important metrics, such as links clicked, reach, and post engagement. The All Ads tab is only useful if you're running more than one ad at a time, and from there, you are able to choose the ad you want to see, and it will give you correspondent metrics, as well as the ability to change the budget for any given ad. The Audiences section is based on the audience you've chosen and allows you to see how many users from that audience you've reached. Here, you can also change your demographic parameters. Lastly, you have the "Automated Ads" tab, but you only have access to it if you've set up automated ads. If you're new to this, using automated ads can really save you time, and if you're just launching ads to get exposure, this might be the best option. However, you don't get to target the audience as accurately as you wish.

The first thing you have to do is create an account with Facebook Ads Manager. Assuming that you already have a business Facebook account (if you don't, you have to create one), go to "Ads Manager," confirm all the information they ask you about in order to set up the page, set a payment mode, and save. Once that's all done, you can enter the Facebook Ads Manager.

The first thing you will see is the dashboard, which will be empty at the time. You will be able to see the overall information about your ads once you've launched at least one. There's a green button on the upper left side of the dashboard that says "Create." Click on it to create a new campaign.

A new menu will pop up that will prompt you to choose the objective of your ad. There are 11 different goals that you can choose from. You have

- store traffic
- catalog sales
- conversions
- brand awareness
- reach
- traffic

- engagement
- app installs
- video views
- lead generation
- messages

Facebook can only start aligning your ad with your goal once you have chosen one. When you have a goal set, you can insert the URL that you want to advertise. Then, Facebook will give you options about what types of ads might be best for you to reach your goal.

The next thing you will be prompted to do is to choose your audience. If you're setting up several ads for the same campaign, you can still choose different segments of your audience to be shown different ads. These are labeled as "Targeting Options," and it might take a little for you to get the right one if you're new to it, but you will get it. The Facebook Ads Manager will give you a tool—a map of the world—where you can narrow down your target audience by choosing the location you want your ad to be shown. Facebook also gives you location suggestions after you've chosen all the options from the list, which is quite large:

- behaviors
- life events
- languages
- work
- education
- financial
- home
- generation
- interests
- connections
- parents
- ethnic affinity

- location
- gender
- age

The software allows you to customize your audience even further by giving you the option to target users who have previously visited the page, are in your contact list, or have used a certain app.

When it comes to setting the budget, Facebook allows you to choose between two options: a daily budget and a lifetime budget. The first is a good option if you want to run your ad at any time during the day by using a daily budget. So, say you have a $5 daily budget, Facebook will pace it throughout the day (keep in mind that the minimum is $1). The lifetime budget option is better used if you want to run your ad for a certain length of time, and Facebook will run the ad only during the amount of time selected.

Now, onto the cost of Facebook ads. As with many other social media platforms, there's no fixed cost, and the price you pay depends on the bidding model and strategy you want to use. According to a study by AdEspresso, this is the average Facebook advertising cost per bidding model:

- cost-per-click (CPC) = $1
- cost-per-like (CPL) = $1.07
- cost-per-download (CPD) = $5.47
- cost-per-thousand-impressions (CPM) = $7.19

When it comes to strategies and bid types, you need to choose the one that suits you best. If you choose "Spend-Based Bidding," which spends all the budget and tries to get you the most value out of it, the strategy here is to reach as many users as possible (within your audience) and maximize valued sales. "Goal-Based Bidding" is a type of bidding that aims to keep things profitable when it comes to spending on ads, but ultimately the goal is to reach your objectives. Essentially, it will try to spend only what is necessary to reach your goals, although it might spend all the budget trying to do so. If compared to "Spend-Based Bidding," the only difference is that it will try not to spend all your budget. Lastly, we have "Manual Bidding," where you can set a maximum bid across all the auctions. There are more advanced options that you can select after you've chosen one of these.

After that, you will have to set a schedule, which essentially lets you choose between running the campaign straight away or scheduling it by adding start and end dates to it. You can also have it run continuously or have it break or be divided. You can even get a little more specific and schedule it to only run certain days of the week or even certain hours.

Then, you can allow Facebook to optimize your bids. You will be prompted to choose whether your bids will target clicks, impressions, or the chosen objective. This is important because it alters the way the software will show your advertising as well as the way you pay for your ads. If you choose to do it this way, the software will display your advertising to more people within your target audience who are more willing to perform the action you want them to do, while the software has control over the bid. If you don't want Facebook to do that, you need to select the "Manual Bidding" option, where you have far more control over the budget.

The next page in the setup is "Delivery." Here, you can choose between "Accelerated" and "Standard." This is just a matter of timing; if you pick "Accelerated," the software will try to get your ads to your audience faster; if you pick "Standard," Facebook will show your ads during the times you've scheduled throughout the day with no specific time.

If you've got your mock-up in Photoshop or any other design program, now's the time to put it to use. The next page on the setup is "Create Your Ad," and here, Facebook also gives you some suggestions on the way you display your ads. If you're looking to link to your page, you have that option, and you will be prompted with two options: links and carousels. The first allows you to show an ad (or a single image), while the other option allows you to show a row of different images (between three and five) that the user can scroll through. Then, once you've chosen the way you want to show your ad, you simply need to upload it. The other ad option you can choose from is "Boost Your Posts." Here, you have more options, such as Mobile News Feed, Desktop Right Column, or Desktop News Feed.

These are all the steps to launch an ad on Facebook. From there, monitoring the performance and retrieving reports will be your task. You can use third-party tools to check the performance metrics of your ads, but you can also use Facebook's. To get a report of your ad's performance, go to the "Analyze and Report" tab, go to "Ads Reporting," and click on "Create Custom Report." You can even choose to get the document in your email.

Launch Your Ad on Instagram

Instagram is owned by Facebook, and because of that, you can use Ads Manager to launch Instagram ads. The process is the same as we've seen for Facebook ads, except when it comes to choosing the platform, you pick Instagram instead of Facebook. There's another way to advertise and launch campaigns on Instagram - through the Instagram app by promoting a post. This is easier than using Ads Manager, and you can pick an existing post you've made (ideally one that is already performing well) and boost it. For that, you will need a business Instagram account as well as a Facebook business page that is linked to that Instagram account.

Click on "Promote" under the post you've already published (it should be in the lower right corner of the post). Then, pick the duration of the ad, the budget you want to use, the audience, and the destination. Click on "Create Promotion," and that's all it takes.

Now, if you're using Ads Manager on Instagram, you have far more ad options. We will go through them all so you can get a better idea of what you can choose.

You have eight different types of ads to choose from on Instagram:

- Reels
- Shopping
- Video
- Image
- Carousel
- IGTV

- Explore
- Collection

Reels Ads

Reels are one of the latest additions when it comes to features on Instagram, and ads are shown between Reels on vertical videos up to 30 seconds. One thing that you should be aware of is the introduction of music or sound in Reels ads. The main goal of Reels ads is for reach, engagement, clicks, awareness, and conversions. Additionally, if you want to add CTA buttons, "Add to Bag" and "View Products" are the best choices.

Shopping Ads

Shopping is big on Instagram, and the app continues to give a lot of attention to this particular niche. It now allows you to purchase products directly from the Instagram app, although you need to change the settings and enable the "Checkout" feature. These ads appear between posts, and with a simple click, they direct the users to the description page of the product. You can also set up the "Shopping Catalog" feature on your account to allow you to run these ads.

The better use for these types of ads is for reach, conversions, awareness, clicks, and engagement.

Video Ads

Video ads appear between posts and can last up to a minute. However, this is usually too long, and users move on to other things, so a 30-second video might be best to keep engagement high. You can use these types of ads for video views, traffic, reach, messages, leads, conversions, awareness, app installs, and engagement. In video ads, you have quite a few CTAs that you can use depending on what you're advertising.

Image Ads

Instagram is an image-based social media platform, so images are unquestionably its strongest suit. With this type of ad, you can promote your products, services, or brands. Choose this type of ad if your promotion is grounded in visuals and you rely on high-quality photos and pictures. While you are allowed to add text, try to keep that to a minimum if you're displaying good-quality images.

When it comes to objectives, you can use image ads for traffic, reach, messages, leads, catalog sales, app installs, awareness, and conversions. It also allows for a long array of CTAs, as well as video ads plus "Open Link," "Request Time," or "See Menu."

Carousel or Stories Ads

You might be familiar with Stories ads, which are similar to Facebook's Carousel ads. This gathers a series of images or videos that the user can swipe to see them. They appear between posts and are a great way to promote. You can use up to 10 videos or images, which is very good if you are promoting a collection, for example.

With these types of ads, you can get reach, traffic to your website, leads, conversions, catalog sales, app installs, awareness, or messages, as well as use the same CTAs you are allowed with Image ads.

IGTV Ads

When a user chooses to use IGTV, you can use video ads to promote your products or services. However, unlike the standard video ads, you can only have videos as long as 15 seconds. They show the IGTV ads in between other IGTV videos, and users are allowed to simply skip them. This type of ad is best used for video views, awareness, reach, and traffic but has a long list of CTAs that you can use.

Explore Ads

The user has to go to the Explore tab to see these ads, and the main function of this is for people to find out about new things such as content, products, or other people and accounts. Also, whatever appears on each user's Explore tab is related to what they follow, which targets exactly what they are looking for. However, accessing the Explore tab is not as easy as other Instagram features since the user has to click on some content, such as a video, image, or post. These ads can be used as videos or images, and they are great for traffic, messages, reach, leads, app installs, awareness, and engagement. The CTAs are the same as for images and videos.

Collection Ads

These types of ads are similar to Shopping and Carousel ads and essentially showcase products or services from Instagram's catalog feature. If you have a brand, this might be one of the best ads you can get, and once clicked by the user, Instagram leads you to more information about the product or service, as well as links the user to checkout if they intend to make a purchase.

Because these ads are quite specific, they are best used for traffic, conversion, and catalog sales, and the only CTAs allowed are "Purchase" and "Learn More."

With this information, you can now choose the ad that best suits your goal. Take into account your strategy and audience, and pick what can get you better results.

Launch Your Ad on Twitter

If Twitter is your platform of choice and you want to garner more followers that eventually will bring in more leads and drive traffic to your website, you need to know how to set up ads on the platform.

With advertising on Twitter, you are able to launch campaigns as well as promote certain Tweets, and much like other platforms, you can choose from a vast array of goals that you want to set for your advertising, such as conversions, app installs, or views. Ideally, you might want to pay for advertising along with your organic traffic to boost more of your campaign. One of the advantages Twitter has when compared to other platforms we've seen so far is that to reach a larger audience, you don't have to spend as much. Alright, so how do you start?

As previously stated, you have the option of using Twitter Ads or Promote Mode, which allows you to promote specific tweets. If you click on "Menu," you can choose between these two options. With promoted tweets, your tweets will come up in searches and streams on the platform for targeted users. Twitter Ads is a little more similar to Facebook Ads Manager, and you usually use more than a single tweet to reach your objective.

If you only want a certain page to get more traffic, perhaps promoting single tweets will get you great results for a fraction of the cost (which is a flat fee every month until you no longer want to promote that tweet). If, on the other hand, you want to increase your followers and raise brand awareness, Twitter Ads is a more comprehensive option.

Let's start with Twitter ads since it is a more complex process. Once you choose that mode, you will be prompted to pick your goal. You have

- awareness
- clicks and conversions
- engagement
- followers
- app installs
- promoted videos
- app re-arrangements
- in-stream video

While most of these options are designed to accomplish your goal of promoting products or services, "followers" focus on promoting your account.

Once you've chosen the goal you want to accomplish, you will need to add some details about the campaign you want to launch. While budget and campaign length are options for every objective you choose, other parameters might differ depending on the type of campaign you choose. Either way, you will have to fill in some information regarding the campaign you're running. Set a daily budget and a total budget, although the latter is up to you. Again, when it comes to spending the money in the budget, you also have two options that are called exactly the same on both Facebook and Instagram Ads Managers: standard or accelerated (they also have the same functionality).

One distinction between this and other ads management social media platforms is that you are required to create an ad group on Twitter first. These are simply individual ads that have their own definitions, such as budget, scheduled times, and even audiences but are part of the same campaign. When you're directed to that page, you will already have an example to the left of your screen, and if you need to create more, you can copy and paste the existing one. This feature gives you a great array of actions for a single campaign. For instance, you might run one ad group for a week using specific ads and targeting specific groups, while in the second week, you use different ads and target a different segment of your audience. However, this will be done in the next steps, but first, choose the bid type.

You have three main options: automatic bid, target bid, and maximum bid. With automatic bids, you allow Twitter to choose the most cost-effective way to reach your audience with the advertising you have. With a target bid, you are the one who sets the budget and how much each ad group gets from that budget. While at maximum bid, you have full control over the cost of your campaign and how much you want to pay every time there's an interaction between your content and your audience.

Still, within the "Details" tab, you can target different audiences to the different ad groups you have. Make sure you target your audience properly because you are paying for it, and mistargeting is just wasted money. Here, you can choose a few parameters such as gender, location, age, language, audience features (audience interests), and device. You can also target by keywords, which is under the "Audience Features" tab, and this feature allows you to target users who have searched for certain keywords that you can add. You can also target based on followers and interests. This can be quite useful if you target a few well-known influencers in your niche. You can do the same for interests, which allows you to target a more broad audience.

The last step in creating, launching, and promoting your Twitter campaign is to choose the creatives (which are single tweets) that you want to advertise along with the specific ad group. Here, you can create new tweets that fit perfectly with the ads you want to run or use existing tweets. If you want to create a new one, click on the blue button on the top right of your page. Before you launch your campaign, you will be directed to a page where you can review every step you've taken to ensure everything is correct. If all looks good, just press "Launch Campaign," and the campaign starts.

To simply use the "promote mode" to highlight a tweet, you can head to the campaign menu and click on "Get started." Choose the tweet you want to promote, the country and time zone you want to promote it in, and then the location and interest as a target. After you've clicked "Proceed," the promotion of the tweet will start.

Launch Your Ad on YouTube

Before we go through how to advertise and launch a campaign on YouTube, there are a few new features that we think are important to point out, as well as the types of ads you can create on YouTube since it's a platform dedicated to the video format.

YouTube is a very different platform to advertise your campaign on, and recently it has made a few changes that are worth pointing out. First, there are more creative restrictions when it comes to the use of copyrighted content, such as music. This also exists on other platforms, but YouTube takes it to another level, and your ads can be taken down if you infringe on such policies.

They've also updated their safety regulations to stop harmful content from reaching their audience, as well as their advertisers on the platform. Things such as clear language and ads with more specific guidelines are also enforced, so even if the content you are trying to advertise is not intended to be harmful, it could be read as if it was, so it's important that you are fully aware of what you can and can't do on the platform.

Another thing that we would like to talk about before we explore YouTube's ads is their cost, which differs a little from other platforms that we've reviewed. YouTube bases its cost on views, and that cost ranges between $0.10 and $0.30 per ad viewed. It also depends on other parameters, such as keywords and niche targets. You can also use keywords as a target, and they are relatively less expensive than on other platforms, costing between $1 and $2 per click. Now that's out of the way, let's start with the types of ads.

There are five types of YouTube ad videos:

- In-Feed Video ads
- Bumper Video ads
- Skippable In-Stream Video ads
- Non-Skippable In-Stream Video ads
- Overlay ads

In-Feed Video Ads

These types of ads appear on the homepage of the user or when they search for videos, as well as related videos. By clicking on it, the user will be directed to another page with more related videos and a banner ad on the right-hand side. These are quite common, but not as specifically targeted as other types.

Bumper Video Ads

These are brief videos, lasting only six seconds. You can usually see them just before you watch a video, and they are not skippable. Because of their short duration, unless these videos can have a great impact on the user, they are quite forgettable. However, when combined with other longer videos, they can really make a great impact. When using Bumper Videos with other types of video ads, make sure you highlight the most important features of the product, service, or brand you want to promote, and with longer videos, you can get into more detail. Think of Bumper Video ads as little reminders.

Skippable In-Stream Video Ads

These are the most common type of video ads on YouTube, and as an advertiser, you only pay for these when the user watches a minimum of 30 seconds or if the user clicks on them. However, these ads can be as short as 12 seconds or as long as 6 minutes, although such a long time is not always recommended since the chances of the user moving on to other things are higher.

These ads will play before the video is selected by the user, but most can be skipped only after 5 or 6 seconds. You can customize your CTAs in your video ads with overlay text. However, there are a few more features that you can add to these video ads. Again, whatever you use in your video ad, from music to people talking, must have the proper copyright or be royalty-free. Since these are skippable videos, your ad needs to be compelling, so users continue to watch, or they will simply skip the video. It's important that you form a narrative that connects with the people and keeps them entertained. That way, your products, services, or brand will be more memorable, increasing engagement. Whether or not users skip your videos, you still have a lot of data to analyze and how to optimize your ads for more engagement.

To get access to this, create a Google Ads account, and some of the metrics you can find there are, for instance, click rates, subscriptions, partial or complete views, and more. All of these metrics should be properly analyzed so you can target your audience better.

Non-Skippable In-Stream Ads

As the name suggests, Non-Skippable Video ads are those that the user cannot skip when selecting a video on YouTube. However, because of that feature, they are a lot shorter, with a duration between 15 and 20 seconds. These are the types of ads that appear when the users are in the middle of a long video (usually longer than 10 minutes).

When it comes to features, you can include the exact same type of features that Skippable Videos offer. As a suggestion, CTAs are better used in these types of ads because the user cannot skip them, and there are more chances of someone clicking on them.

Overlay Ads

These ads are becoming more common on YouTube videos, and they are simple banners that usually appear at the bottom of the videos the user is watching. While on their own, they might not do much, when combined with other types of ads, they can make an impact. As such, if you don't want your advertising to be intrusive to your audience, these are the best options.

Setting Up

Now that you know everything there is to know about the different types of YouTube ads, it's time to find out how to actually launch the ad and the campaign. First create your advertisement. There are many different tools that you can use that are not too difficult to get started with. For example, one of those programs is Animoto, where you can simply choose a template (or you can start from scratch), add clips and images, and customize as you wish. It's quite a powerful tool that can create a professional video even if you're just starting out. Another common software to use is a combination of QuickTime to record and Photo Booth or iMovie to create the video. There are plenty of video tutorials online for whatever tool you end up choosing. Once you've got your video done, here's how you set up your campaign.

The first step is quite easy; simply upload your video through your YouTube account. It's a simple drag-and-drop, so there's not much to it. Before you can create your campaign, you will need to set up your Google Ads account (or log in if you already have one).

As you start, the first page that comes up will ask you to create a new campaign. Look for a button that says "Set Up Without Creating a Campaign." The tool will lead you to the Google Ads dashboard. Then, you can go for the "New Campaign" button.

Then, you will be prompted to pick the goal as well as the type of campaign you want to use. When it comes to goals, you will have the option to pick "leads," "sales," "brand awareness," "website traffic," "product and brand consideration," "app promotion," "local store visits and promotions," or to create a campaign without guidance. Then, you can pick between two different campaign types: "Display," where you can have different types of ads run across the web, and "Video," where you focus more on engagement and reaching on YouTube.

After that, choose your strategy and subtype of the campaign. In the campaign subtype, you can choose between three: video reach campaign, ad sequence, or out stream. For the purpose of advertising and running a campaign, choose the first. Then comes the strategy. This is only the way you'd like to get to your goal, and you have another two options: "Efficient Reach," where you can use some of the types of video ads we've talked about, such as Skippable In-Stream, Bumper, or a mix of both; or "Non-Skippable In-Stream," where you can use non-skippable videos as the name suggests.

After that, you will get to choose the name of the campaign. This is a fairly simple step, especially if you already know what your campaign is going to be called. Below that, you will have the bid strategy, but for now, don't change it. It should be set as "Target CPM."

Moving on to the budget, here you can also choose to set a budget for the day (or each day of the campaign) or set it for the whole campaign. Again, if you want to be on top of how much you're spending, we suggest sticking to a daily budget. This is so you don't spend all your money in the first few days and have nothing left for the remainder of the campaign. However, if you set a total budget, YouTube won't spend more than what you've set. On the same screen, you will be prompted to pick a start and an end date for your campaign.

Continuing with the setup, get more specific about where you want your ads to show. You'll have three different options here: YouTube videos, YouTube search results, and video partners on the display network. The first allows you to show your ads before or in the middle of YouTube videos; in the YouTube search results, as the name suggests, on the search result pages when people search for videos, but also on the YouTube homepage and channel pages. And with the video partners on the display network option, you can have your ads appear on video pages (usually around or under the videos all across the Google Network). If you do want to pick different ways of showing your ads, we suggest that you create different campaigns because it's a lot easier to track your metrics this way. After that, you can select the user's location, who you want the ads to appear with, and the language they speak.

You have the option to pick what types of videos you want your ads to be shown on. So, if certain videos have sexual content, gore, or profanity, you can choose not to show ads on those videos. You can click on "Expanded Inventory" if you don't want your ads to show in videos with unreasonable sexual content, profanity, or graphic content; "Standard Inventory" to exclude videos that have quite some graphic content or profanity; and "Limited Inventory" if you don't want your ads to be shown in videos with low to moderate sexual content or profanity. You also have more options to exclude your ads from other types of videos, such as live streams or videos based on labels.

Then, you can move on to the advanced settings. While this is not mandatory to go through, it can customize your campaign even further. For instance, you could choose different operating systems on which you want your ads to be shown (which is quite good if you're only doing mobile ads), create a custom schedule with interruptions, and more.

The next step is to set up audience segments and demographics. There's a long list when it comes to demographics, with several options. Gender, age, parental status, and even household income are all factors. In the audience segment, you can pick more detailed interests that your audience might have, such as food and dining, video games, etc. After that, pick target keywords, placements, and topics. This is a continuation of the previous set, where you picked your audience. You can filter them by keywords or topics, and your ads will only appear to people who fall into that category. Test different types of keywords until you find the one that gives you more leads, clicks, and overall engagement. You can also pick an audience segment that has already, in one way or another, been in contact with your products or services.

When all of that is done, you can start bidding. Essentially, you will set up a maximum cost that you want to pay for a single view of your ad. Then, one of the last steps is to add the link to your video ad so it can run on YouTube. There are two options here: an in-stream or in-display ad. While the first will run smoothly before or in the middle of the videos, with the second you will add a description and a title.

That's it. Then you can link your Google Ads account so you can track your metrics. Simply go to settings, set up, and link accounts.

Tips to Optimize Your YouTube Ads

Because it's a little different to optimize video ads than it is to optimize images or any other type of ad, we will give you some tips on how you can do it.

As with any optimization, you need to define your metrics and objectives. With video ads, there are four parameters that are quite important: audience, views and impressions, conversion, and view rate.

The audience is the same for other types of ads that you track. You can check their gender, income, age, etc. Views and impressions mean that you can track an increase or decrease in views and how that segment of the audience ended up seeing the ads. Conversions are the same in other types of ads and tell you how many people or leads actually generated income. Lastly, the view rate determines how engaging your ad is. Essentially, it tells you how many people watched the video ad until the end.

To better optimize your video ads, address those low-performing placements you have. For instance, if you chose to run ads all over the Google Network, you can simply go to "Video Targeting," "Placements," and "Where Ads are Shown" and check where your ads have been underperforming. This way, you can pick other places to place your ads. Another great tip is to use a thumbnail image, preferably a custom one to be more precise. This is an image that attracts the user to click on it and show your ad. However, make sure it's a high-quality image and that it actually entices people to click on it.

Creating a YouTube ending slate is another great tip that you can do. Essentially, these are end screens that link to your pages or subscription buttons after videos are played. This is great because, if a user has seen the whole video, they are sure to be interested in related topics, which might include your product, service, or brand, and so are more likely to click on it.

Negative remarketing is for advertisers that, despite running a long campaign, want to bring in more subscribers and so can come up with a few parameters to choose an audience segment that they are yet to reach. Using transcriptions or closed captions in your videos can make a remarkable difference in the quality of your videos and ads. However, these are better placed if you're creating video content. This is because, although Google does generate automatic captions on YouTube videos, they are a little sketchy. If you have high-quality ones, a target audience that might not be fluent in the language of the video will certainly appreciate it and continue to watch your content.

That's enough information about YouTube video ads to get you started. There are a lot more things that we could be discussing, but that would probably take a whole other book. If you're interested in knowing more, there are tons of interesting video tutorials all over the web to further your knowledge on the topic.

Launch Your Ad on LinkedIn

LinkedIn is a great platform to connect in a more professional way; however, if the product or service that you want to promote falls within this category, then LinkedIn is a great way to promote it.

And while this platform doesn't completely diverge in the way it approaches advertising from other platforms that we've been reviewing, it has its own tools and its own audience. Let's delve into how exactly everything works. LinkedIn ads have five main steps that you need to follow before you start advertising your campaign. These are picking your objective, choosing criteria for your targets, choosing the format of the ad, setting a budget, and measuring your ad's performance. Until now, there have not been that many differences compared with other ad platforms.

The first step in this LinkedIn advertising process is to create your LinkedIn ad campaign. Even if you already have an account with LinkedIn, go to the LinkedIn Marketing Solutions platform (which is a different website) and click on "Create Ad." Then, sign up and create a Campaign Manager account. You will be taken to the homepage of your campaign manager account, where you will see the button "Create Campaign" on the upper right-hand side of the page. However, you will need to enter your billing information if you haven't already done so before you can access the dashboard. They will prompt you to add a name for your campaign and a campaign group. These groups are like those Twitter ad groups; they're just to make it easier for you and keep things organized. In fact, you don't even have to create a new group; you can simply use the default group that is already there.

After you've done that, the next step is to set ad campaign goals. While you have three main objective groups, under each of those you have more to choose from. The three main ones are awareness, which only has a single subgroup called "brand awareness," and consideration, which has three other subgroups: "website visits," "engagement," and "video views." Lastly, you have the third group called conversions, with four different subgroups to choose from: "lead generation," "website conversions," "job applicants," and "talent leads." Essentially, by choosing some of these, you will help LinkedIn customize your ad campaign and tailor it to different audience segments, as well as increase the ROI.

Even if some of the parameters above already narrow down some of the audience your ads will be shown to, the next step will really focus on the audience segment you want to target. This step is similar to all the other platforms we've seen, where you can pick the age range of the audience, their interests, the devices used, etc.

After that, choose your ad format. LinkedIn allows you to choose between four different types: sponsored content, message ads, dynamic ads, and text ads. Let's go through them.

Sponsored content is all around the user's news feed, in between other posts and content. They come in three different formats: single images, videos, and carousels. If you remember, a carousel can be a sequence of images or videos that the user can swipe through. Then you've got message ads, which are shown in the user's inbox. These are great if you really want certain segments of your audience to read your ads directly. These are also great to measure since you have defined trends between those who open the message and those who don't.

The next are dynamic ads, and these are highly customized ads that only appear if the user is using LinkedIn through a desktop. The ad will appear differently to each member of your audience based on their data. They also come in three different formats: Job ads, which you can use if you want to promote a certain job; Spotlight ads, which advertise offers; and Follower ads, which advertise your page on LinkedIn.

Lastly, there are Text ads, which appear on the right sidebar of the user's platform and are quite simple. All they have is a little text under it with an image (usually a logo). These are great for raising awareness and boosting other types of ads within your campaign.

After you've chosen your type of ad, you can then choose your ad placement. Different placements will give your advertising more or less exposure within the LinkedIn platform as well as its third-party ones, although the option to advertise on third-party platforms is not available for all the types of ads we've discussed. You can leave out some placements if you don't feel they will add anything to your campaign.

The next step is to budget and schedule. If it's your first time using LinkedIn and you are still figuring out your audience, we suggest setting a daily budget so you can see after a few days if it's working or not with the chosen audience. If your campaign is going well, you can either set a total budget or increase your daily ad budget. You will then be prompted to pick a schedule, where you can set a start and an end date.

On to the bid type, and here you will have three options: maximum cost-per-click (CPC) bid, maximum pay-per-thousand impressions (CPM) bid, and automated bid. We've been through other platforms that offered the same types of bids. But just go through them quickly to refresh your memory. A CPC bid will charge every time a user clicks on your ad; with a CPM bid, LinkedIn charges you after your ad is seen by 1,000 people, regardless of whether they have clicked on or interacted with your ad. Furthermore, the CPM bid is not available for use with LinkedIn third-party partners. Lastly, you have the automated bid, where LinkedIn determines the amount as long as it maximizes your ad campaign.

While it's not easy to pick between these options, you should try to determine your end goal and what type of bid will grant you more exposure. There might be some trying out different strategies if this is your first time advertising on the platform, but you will quickly get the hang of it. Also, as always, don't forget to set up the conversion tracking on the platform so you can measure your ads' and campaigns' performance.

Although these are all the major steps, you haven't launched your campaign and advertised it yet. Even though you have picked your parameters, and your ads for the campaign, you still need to Click on "Create a New Ad for This Campaign". After you've chosen the image or video, LinkedIn will show you different layouts of the same ad and campaign. Before that, you will have to add some information, such as the size of the ad image or video, a headline, a description, and a destination URL. After that, you will see the previews and pick the one that you'd like to have. Click "Create," and that's done. You will be led back to the main dashboard, where you can start another campaign or add more ads to the existing campaign if you want. Your ads won't appear straight away on your audience's pages because LinkedIn takes a little to review your ads and campaign.

Again, and like most ad platforms, make sure you create a buyer persona, create great CTAs, add value to your ads, and test before you spend all of your budgets.

Launch Your Ad on Google

If you want to expand your audience without having a specific platform in mind, Google might be the best place for it. To start, you first need to get Google Ads to manage your promotions. What's interesting about Google is that your ads could go across several platforms, such as YouTube or Blogger.

A word of caution: because Google is such a vast platform, you may need to experiment with a different approach to make it effective. Because your ads will certainly appear on Google's search engine page, you should avoid broad keyword terms. This means that you choose to really think about the keywords you will use, although changing them as you start your campaign is also something that you could practice. Since so many people use the Google search engine, broad keywords are more likely to be displayed to the wrong people, which, at the end of the day, might be money badly spent. Again, make sure you understand what is working and what is not so you can make changes appropriately.

Make sure the ad you're running is relevant to the search intent of your target audience, or you won't get the desired performance. This means that every part of the ad, including the copy and the headline, has to be in sync with the keywords you're bidding on. Also, make sure the solution you're presenting solves the problem of the audience you're targeting. This way, you can be certain that you will achieve the desired results.

You will also want to make sure you understand what Quality Score (QS) is—Google's rank—and how you can improve it, so your ads rank better. Essentially, the better Quality Score you have, the higher ad placements you will have on the SERP. The lower it is, the less people get to see your ad. Google allows you to see your QS, so make sure you can improve it to maximize the money you're spending.

Optimizing your landing page will definitely help. Not only will it help you rank better on SERP, but it will also keep your audience coming back to you since you have a much better landing page. Most affiliate marketers and brands focus too much on getting clicks and too little on the overall audience experience. They should make sure everything is high-quality from the moment the audience interacts with your ad, brand, or product until they purchase it.

When we compare Google to other ad platforms, there are a few concepts that stand out. For instance, AdRank is the metric used by Google to figure out where your ad will be placed (in ranking order). The higher it is, the more people are able to see it. This is determined by QS and the value of your bid.

The display network might also be something that you're not familiar with, but we've briefly mentioned it when talking about YouTube ads. Essentially, if your ads are on the Google Display Network (GDN), they can appear in the search result pages of Google, YouTube, Blogger, and any other platform that is linked with the GDN.

Ad extensions allow you to add more information to your advertising for free, and there are five different categories of ad extensions: app, offer, sitelink, location, and call. App extensions add a link to your ad on the SERP, but only on mobile devices. If you have an app to advertise, this is an excellent choice for an extension. An offer extension only happens if you have a promotion going, and it adds a little more information to an offer to entice users to click on it. A sitelink extension simply extends your ad and gives you an additional link. A location extension adds a location to your ad as well as your phone number, which is great if you have a company and want to advertise it. And lastly, a call extension also allows you to add a phone number.

QS is determined by the keyword chosen, the CTR, and the quality of your landing page, and it is what determines your AdRank rank.

There are five types of ad campaigns on Google: display, search, shopping, apps, and video. You can only choose one of these ad types per campaign. A display ad campaign focuses on broadening your audience because it shows you ads through the GDN. Here, you pay per impression or click. However, your ads can be shown to a much broader audience (even if they are not as accurate as other forms of advertising).

Search ad campaigns are among the most popular with Google, and they appear as text on search results pages. This is a great type of campaign if you are looking to get eyeballs on your ads because these ads will be shown with organic searches. There is a variation of these types of ads called "Responsive Search Ads," and you can add more than one version of your ad copy and headline, and the Google algorithm then chooses the one that is ranking better on the SERP.

Shopping ad campaigns are also visible on SERPs and provide the user with product information as well as other details such as price. You can use a secondary tool called Google Merchant Center, where you have to add information about the product you are advertising so it appears on the ad. This type of campaign is great if you want to promote a product instead of your brand.

App ad campaigns simply advertise mobile applications. These are not only run on the SERP but also on Google Play, YouTube, GDN, and more. However, you don't have to come up with a design for this ad or campaign; you can simply add information about the app, and the algorithm does the rest. Lastly, video ad campaigns work in a similar way to YouTube ads: when the users type certain keywords, the ad pops up on the search results page.

To use Google Ads, you first need to set up your Google Ads account, which you can do by going to the website and clicking on "Start Now." Choose a business name and a URL for your website (make sure the URL is correct since it is the link your audience will click on when your ad shows up).

Then, the next step is to choose your goal. You have four different options: get website calls and sign-ups; get more visits; get more calls; or get more views on YouTube. After you've picked your advertising goals, create your ad. This might be a little challenging since it requires some creativity to come up with something good right away, so take your time here. Google also provides some tips on the page that you can review. You will have three headlines and two descriptions to write for your advertising.

After that, add keywords that are related to your products, services, or brand. Then, click on "Next," and you will be prompted to set the location of your ad. You can pick more than one location for your ad to be shown. Google also displays a map for your convenience.

The next step is setting your budget. With Google Ads, it works a little differently since they present you with a few options according to the information you have given them so far. These options will tell you the daily average spent, the monthly maximum spent, and the estimated number of clicks each month. Next, add your payment details and click "Submit."

To get more information about your performance, link your Google Analytics account to your Google Ads account. It's quite simple to use, and it will make a big difference when looking at your performance.

One more important thing about Google Ads is their bidding system, where you can choose between automated and manual bidding. An automated bidding system allows Google to make its own decisions, which are based on your competitors' performance and decisions as well. If you're choosing this method, it's best that you set a maximum budget and let Google work it out with what it has. With manual bidding, set your bid amounts for the different ad groups you have, as well as keywords.

Checklist

☐	Choose your target audience
☐	Choose the platform(s) for your ad(s)
☐	Decide on an advertising budget
☐	Create your message
☐	Decide whether you will advertise for brand awareness OR product awareness first
☐	Create test ads
☐	Create creative assets
☐	Launch advertising campaign

Conclusion

That's it! That's how to get started with your affiliate marketing career. Keep in mind that although this is a very comprehensive book about affiliate marketing for beginners and you will have a good knowledge foundation on the topic, there is always something else to learn, especially because the affiliate marketing industry is still quite young, so every time technology advances, there are things to be learned. Adapt a growth mindset and learn more to become better at what you do and to not only use affiliate marketing as a side hustle but actually do it as a full-time job, if that's what you want, of course.

If you remember, the affiliate marketing ecosystem has four main characters at play: the merchant that pays you (the affiliate marketer) to get their products, services, or brand promoted to their audience; the affiliate marketer (you) who promotes products or services from the merchant to their audience; the affiliate network or program that connects affiliate marketers with merchants; and the customer who is at the end of the cycle and purchases the products or services the affiliate marketer promotes from the merchant. When putting this in context, we get the different stages of affiliate marketing.

You, the affiliate marketer, placed the affiliate link into your content. This link takes the customer to the merchant's product or service page, where the customer can purchase the product or service. After the purchase is made, the affiliate link is tracked back to the affiliate marketer, and the merchant pays a commission (sometimes, the affiliate marketer can get commissions from simpler actions that don't require the customer to purchase the item but, for example, to visit the merchant's web page or to simply click on the link).

To get started with affiliate marketing, create a content website (unless you choose to do unaffiliated affiliate marketing). This content website can be anything from a blog to a social media page to a YouTube channel, etc., as long as you can promote affiliate links or the merchant's products or services. Before that, choose your niche. This will often change how you create your content for your website or for your social media pages since it has to relate to the niche in question and the products or services that you are going to sell. For this, conduct meticulous research to find a breach in the market where you can make money in an oversaturated niche. After that, create content for your website and keep it updated, as well as optimize it and track your performance and your ranks.

Getting the best affiliate program is also important since it will contribute to your success. There are many types out there, and we've covered the main ones. Choosing the right one will depend on what you are promoting, but make sure you get the most out of these programs and don't fall into a trap. Always ensure that they pay on time, and it's even better if they reward their top affiliate marketers. Ideally, you want to move on to work directly with brands so you can cut out the middleman, but for that, you first need to gain experience and a reputation. However, send inquiries to brands that are within your niche, and perhaps you will get a deal with one of them. It's important to know exactly what you are doing. It will shape your content accordingly. For instance, if you want to get clicks on your affiliate links or if you want conversions instead, there are also many types of affiliate marketers to choose from, such as influencer/social media affiliate marketers, bloggers, those who focus solely on mobile marketing, affiliate email marketers, etc.

We have dedicated two chapters to strategies and tools that we won't cover here, but make sure you start out with the beginner's ones and move on to more complex ones. Again, understand the easier ones so you can perform the more complex strategies, but that doesn't mean you won't use the beginner strategies during your career as an affiliate marketer even after years of experience. These strategies have been tested for several years, and they still work, so make sure you understand the basics. The same is true for tools. While there are new tools coming out almost every month, all the ones we've covered here are reliable and will help you reach your goals.

In the last two chapters, we've parted ways slightly from a sole affiliate marketing perspective and branched out to more of a merchant point of view. However, everything that we've talked about, including how to launch and advertise your campaign, can be used not only by a brand wanting to expand its audience but also if you want to project your brand as an affiliate marketer, which is especially important if you want to make direct deals with brands.

Being an affiliate marketer is very exciting, and there's always something new to learn. You have in this book more than enough tools to not only start but succeed in the industry, but it will take hard work and persistence; however, the gains can be immense.

Before you go, we just wanted to say thank you for purchasing our book. You could have picked from dozens of other books on the same topic but you took a chance and chose this one. So, a HUGE thanks to you for getting this book and for reading all the way to the end.

Now, we wanted to ask you for a small favor. COULD YOU PLEASE CONSIDER POSTING A REVIEW ON THE PLATFORM? (Reviews are one of the easiest ways to support the work of independent authors.)

This feedback will help us continue to write the type of books that will help you get the results you want. So if you enjoyed it, please let us know!

We wish you much Success on your Journey!

www.ingramcontent.com/pod-product-compliance
Lightning Source LLC
Chambersburg PA
CBHW030117100526
44591CB00009B/428